EAST ANGLIAN ARCHAEOLOGY

Standards for Field Archaeology in the East of England

by David Gurney

with contributions by
Stewart Bryant, Jenny Glazebrook,
Andy Hutcheson, Peter Murphy,
Ben Robinson and Jonathan Smith

East Anglian Archaeology
Occasional Paper No.14, 2003

Association of Local Government Archaeological Officers
East of England Region

EAST ANGLIAN ARCHAEOLOGY
OCCASIONAL PAPER NO.14

EAST OF ENGLAND

Published by
ALGAO (East of England region)
Algao.cji@ntlworld.com

Enquiries about the *Regional Standards* should be addressed to
Archaeology and Environment
Union House
Gressenhall
Dereham
Norfolk NR20 4DR

Editor: David Gurney
Managing Editor: Jenny Glazebrook

Editorial Sub-committee:
Brian Ayers, Archaeology and Environment Officer, Norfolk Museums and Archaeology Service
David Buckley, County Archaeologist, Essex Planning Department
Keith Wade, Archaeological Service Manager, Suffolk County Council
Peter Wade-Martins
Stanley West

Set in Times Roman by Jenny Glazebrook using Corel Ventura™
Printed by Witley Press Ltd., Hunstanton, Norfolk

ISBN 0 9510695 5 1

For details of *East Anglian Archaeology Occasional Papers*, see back cover

The *Regional Standards* have been published with funding from English Heritage, and the counties of the
East of England region: Bedfordshire, Cambridgeshire, Essex, Hertfordshire, Norfolk and Suffolk

Cover picture:
The Ordnance Survey benchmark on the Union Workhouse, Gressenhall
Photo: David Gurney

Contents

List of Contributors

Stewart Bryant
County Archaeologist, Hertfordshire County Council

Jenny Glazebrook
Managing Editor, *East Anglian Archaeology*

David Gurney
Principal Landscape Archaeologist, Norfolk Museums
and Archaeology Service

Andy Hutcheson
Development Control Archaeologist, Norfolk Museums
and Archaeology Service

Peter Murphy
English Heritage Regional Advisor for Archaeological
Science, Centre of East Anglian Studies, University of
East Anglia

Ben Robinson
Archaeological Officer, Peterborough City Council

Jonathan Smith
Planning Archaeologist, Hertfordshire County Council

Acronyms

Acknowledgements

Thanks are due to the contributors to this document, and to the members of the Association of Local Government Archaeological Officers in the East of England (including English Heritage) who, together with their archaeological development control officers, provided a great deal of useful help and advice during its preparation. In particular, Richard Havis (Essex County Council) devoted much effort to the document and its application in the development control/planning context. Thanks are also due to the archaeological contractors and consultants currently working in the region for their many helpful comments on the consultation draft, and colleagues within the Norfolk Museums and Archaeology Service for their support and encouragement, especially Brian Ayers, County Archaeologist for Norfolk. The cartoons which illuminate the text have been drawn by Piers Wallace.

Preface

Following extensive consultation, this document was formally adopted by the Committee of the Association of Local Government Archaeological Officers for the East of England at Bury St Edmunds on 12 September 2002. It was also agreed that it would be fully reviewed after 2–3 years, and that the Committee would receive regular reports on its implementation and comments received. These can be sent to the author at Norfolk Landscape Archaeology, Union House, Gressenhall, Dereham, Norfolk NR20 4DR or by email to david.gurney@norfolk.gov.uk.

A copy of this document is also available as a PDF file, on the web at www.eaareports.org.uk.

Foreword

by Stewart Bryant

The Committee of the Association of Local Government Archaeological Officers for the East of England has produced this document. It aims to fulfill the following key objectives:

- to provide a quick reference guide on standards applicable to archaeological fieldwork and subsequent activities, including development-led projects, research projects and amateur (non-vocational) activities. This has been organised thematically for ease of reference in the widest possible range of contexts, and with a bibliography of the main sources. The document is to be kept under review and revised and updated as necessary.

- to provide a statement of the philosophy of the Committee regarding field archaeology, especially the importance of standards and research frameworks.

- to implement Planning Policy Guidance in the region, with particular regard to securing the evaluation of archaeological sites prior to determination of planning applications in line with PPG16.

- to improve the standard of archaeological fieldwork and the quality of research in the East of England by stating the principles that underpin decisions made by archaeological advisors to Local Planning Authorities.

- to provide details of methodological fieldwork requirements in key areas, and a benchmark against which archaeological projects can be monitored and assessed.

However, the document is not intended as a comprehensive guide to standards or as the minimum requirement for standards and as such should not be used by itself as guidance for the preparation of Project Designs or Written Schemes of Investigation. These documents should always be based upon the specific and detailed requirements of Briefs produced for individual projects, supported by and with reference to (where appropriate) these generic regional standards and Institute of Field Archaeologists standards and guidance.

- to move towards a greater clarity and consistency of approach across the region in terms of fieldwork methodology, fieldwork standards and the decision-making process for development-related archaeological projects, at the same time recognising that the variable nature of the landscape, the development context and the archaeological record will necessarily always result in some differences of approach.

Introduction

The Development of Regional Standards for Field Archaeology in the East of England

Across the East of England region, archaeologists working within Local Government are responsible for providing archaeological advice to Local Planning Authorities (LPAs), developers (and their archaeological consultants) and a wide range of other bodies whose actions may have an impact on the historic environment.

The Association of Local Government Archaeological Officers for the East of England (ALGAOEE) seeks to safeguard the historic environment by providing advice to LPAs on the archaeological implications of development proposals, and by ensuring that archaeological work within the region is conducted to the highest possible standard during fieldwork, analysis and publication of results. Their committee has prepared a Regional Action Plan, one objective of which is to *develop consistent approaches in the region to the preservation and management of the historic environment within the planning framework* (Association of Local Government Officers East of England Regional Committee 2000, 22–23).

The national Association of Local Government Archaeological Officers has also published a *Strategy 2001–2006* (2001), and its aims with reference to Field Archaeology are:

- to support the development of good professional practice in the monitoring of archaeological fieldwork, ensuring that work is carried out to appropriate briefs and specifications;

- to promote the framing of all projects within the context of national and local research agendas;

- to work in partnership with the Institute of Field Archaeologists (IFA) to ensure that professional standards are maintained throughout the archaeological contracting sector.

Within these national and regional contexts, the primary aim of this document is *to promote best practice in archaeological work in the region, and to assist professional archaeologists, developers and their appointed professional archaeological consultants and contractors with the provision of high standards of data collection and report preparation.* Although principally targeted at, and of use with reference to, archaeological fieldwork generated by the planning/development control process, its contents are broadly applicable to all field archaeology projects undertaken by professional or amateur (non-vocational) archaeologists and for this reason it has been arranged thematically.

The standards and practices that are documented here are based upon well-established techniques and procedures developed in the region since the early 1970s, and the first county standards document produced within the region (Norfolk Landscape Archaeology 1998). Expressed as a set of statements provided separately from Project Briefs, these *Regional Standards* now define required policy for work within the East of England region

to which archaeological contractors and consultants (and others) are expected to adhere. They also provide a manual of procedures that should reflect common practice familiar to competent professional and amateur archaeologists.

It is certainly not the intention that the production of *Regional Standards* should stifle debate or discourage innovation, and it is hoped that archaeological contractors and consultants will continue to introduce new and alternative approaches and techniques in order to meet the wider objectives of Project Designs (also known as Method Statements or Written Schemes of Investigations) or Project Specifications.

It is expected that all Project Designs prepared by archaeological contractors or consultants will state that all works will be carried out in full accordance with the Brief provided by the LGAO and, where required by the Brief, these *Regional Standards*. Where alternative approaches or techniques are proposed, these should not be employed without the prior written approval of the relevant LGAO.

Archaeological contractors and consultants should note that these *Regional Standards* stipulate basic *methodological* standards. It is considered axiomatic that all will strive to achieve the highest possible *qualitative* standards and apply the most advanced and appropriate techniques possible within a context of continuous improvement. A primary aim will be to maximise the recovery of archaeological data and thereby contribute to the development of a greater understanding of the historic environment. Monitoring officers will therefore seek and expect clear evidence of commitment to the historic resource of the East of England, with Project Designs being drawn up within a context of added value.

Thus the *Regional Standards* are intended to complement the regional *Research Frameworks*, which are vitally important in setting the broad parameters for individual projects and ensuring their relevance to wider archaeological endeavour.

They also provide an explicit framework within which the quality of archaeological project work may be assessed. Obviously some aspects of the archaeological resource vary considerably across the region, and so local requirements as expressed in Briefs and Specifications will always take precedence. Nevertheless, developers, contractors and consultants working in the region have a right to expect some basic consistency in curatorial approaches across administrative boundaries.

Adherence to defined standards alone, of course, does not guarantee the success of archaeological projects. Archaeological work is concerned with discovery and demands that investigative approaches are examined critically, and modified if necessary, in response to circumstances that unfold in the field. Recognition of exceptional evidence, anomalous evidence, or comparative evidence and the adoption of correct techniques for its treatment, is dependent upon good national, regional, and local contextual knowledge. Agreed standards, however, at least provide a vital part of a common dialogue within which consensus regarding approaches to particular archaeological tasks may be reached.

Archaeological advisors within local government seek to create a framework of knowledge and co-operation within which successful development-led and other archaeological projects can occur, and it is in this spirit that the *Regional Standards* have been adopted.

Professional Values in Development-Led Archaeological Work
by Ben Robinson

ALGAOEE considers that all development-led investigative archaeological work should make a contribution to archaeological research and to the understanding of the past.

ALGAOEE considers that all investigative archaeological work should be undertaken to achieve maximum value within project resources. The value of a project will be determined by the informational outcome — the comprehensiveness of the record created, contribution to the archaeological knowledge base, and contribution to public promotional/educational output.

ALGAOEE acknowledges the value of a thorough understanding (by archaeological contractors, consultants and curatorial staff) of the local and regional archaeological environment.

ALGAOEE welcomes new approaches to archaeological investigation and the generation of new research questions by all those with an interest in the region's archaeology, where these have been formulated through a thorough consideration of the region's archaeological resources.

ALGAOEE encourages the participation of all those with an interest in the region's archaeology in promotional effort, public events and exhibitions, research seminars, and educational initiatives.

ALGAOEE encourages the dissemination of information regarding the region's archaeology within local, regional and national publications.

ALGAOEE acknowledges the value of programmes for the professional development of staff within curatorial sections, contracting organisations and archaeological consultancies. The presence of such programmes and their demonstrable efficacy in regard to approaches to regional archaeology are an essential part of organisational development.

ALGAOEE welcomes beneficial initiatives and partnership between the region's voluntary and professional archaeological communities.

ALGAOEE expects all members of project teams to display an awareness of the local and regional archaeological context for their work. This awareness will be commensurate with their responsibilities within the project team.

ALGAOEE members recognise their responsibility to ensure that staff taking on development control advisory duties and a monitoring role for contractual work, are informed of the wider national, regional, and local archaeological context of their advice. It is their responsibility to ensure that advisory staff maintain awareness of national, regional and local research priorities.

ALGAOEE members have a responsibility to ensure the validity and integrity of development control advice and powers exercised within a monitoring role.

ALGAOEE members will encourage their staff with advisory and monitoring roles to participate fully in local and regional research effort or technical development.

ALGAOEE members will encourage the flow of archaeological information between LGAOs, Sites and Monuments Records, Historic Environment Records, Urban Archaeological Databases and archaeological consultants and contractors. They should ensure that archaeological knowledge and information is disseminated equitably to all organisations and individuals with a legitimate interest in the region's past.

Planning Guidance and the Historic Environment

Archaeology and Planning (PPG16)

In November 1990, the Department of the Environment published *Planning Policy Guidance 16 Archaeology and Planning* (PPG16), which sets out the Secretary of State's policy on archaeological remains on land and how they should be preserved or recorded. It describes how archaeological remains are a finite and non-renewable resource, highly vulnerable to damage and destruction, and gives advice on the handling of archaeological remains and discoveries under the development plan and control system, including the weight to be given to them in planning decisions and the use of planning conditions. Where nationally important remains and their settings are affected by proposed development, there should be a presumption in favour of their physical preservation.

PPG16 also firmly establishes that archaeology is a material consideration in the assessment by a Local Planning Authority (LPA) of a planning application, and that 'it is reasonable for the Planning Authority to request the prospective developer to arrange for an archaeological field evaluation to be carried out before any decision on the planning application is taken' (PPG 16, para 21). On this basis, the impact of the proposed development on the historic environment can be assessed and an informed and reasonable planning decision can then be taken.

On sites where the physical preservation *in situ* of archaeological remains is not justified, LPAs will satisfy themselves before granting planning permission that the developer has made appropriate and satisfactory provision for the excavation and recording of the remains. This is normally secured by the imposition of an appropriate planning condition (a negative or 'Grampian' condition) in line with *The Use of Conditions in Planning Permissions* (Department of the Environment/Welsh Office Circular 11/95, Appendix A, paras 53–55), or an agreement under Section 106 of the *Town and County Planning Act 1990*. In these cases, a mitigation strategy will be devised to safeguard the archaeological remains by means of engineering solutions, by redesign to preserve any remains *in situ*, or by the excavation of any remains and their replacement 'by record'.

Environmental Impact Assessment (EIA) Directives and Regulations are also highly relevant to management of the historic environment, as these require EIAs to be carried out, before development consent is granted, for certain types of projects which are judged likely to have significant environmental effects (see Directives 85/337/EEC and 97/11/EC, *Note on Environmental Impact Assessment Directive for Local Planning Authorities (1999 EIA Regulations)* (Office of the Deputy Prime Minister 2002) and *Environmental Impact Assessment* (DETR Circular 02/99)).

Terrestrial and marine archaeological remains provide a seamless physical and intellectual continuum. The management of archaeological remains under water (including inland waters, estuaries and ports, intertidal areas and the territorial sea) will generally require specialist advice and non-standard procedures. Government advice on coastal planning for local authorities is given in *Planning Policy Guidance Note 20, Coastal Planning* (Department of the Environment/Welsh Office 1992), and English Heritage and the Royal Commission on the Historical Monuments of England have published a useful statement (1996).

There are also various codes of practice for particular forms of development, such as mineral sites (Confederation of British Industry 1991) or seabed developments (Joint Nautical Archaeology Policy Committee 1995).

Works affecting Scheduled Ancient Monuments or their settings will require Scheduled Monument Consent, and in these cases English Heritage must be contacted.

The Built Environment (PPG15)

In September 1994, The Department of the Environment and the Department of National Heritage also produced *Planning Policy Guidance Note 15, Planning and the Historic Environment* (PPG15). This provides a full statement of Government policies for the identification and protection of historic buildings, conservation area and other elements of the historic environment. It complements the guidance on archaeology given in PPG16 and makes provision for the appropriate assessment of the archaeological implications and for programmes of recording of historic buildings.

Some standing structures are Scheduled Ancient Monuments (SAMs) and/or Listed Buildings. The overwhelming majority of the built environment, however, is not covered by such designations. Despite this, many do retain an archaeological significance. It is important that this is identified at the earliest opportunity and that appropriate decisions are taken by the LPA on the advice of the LGAO and/or other specialist advisers when a standing structure is faced with a development proposal, demolition or, in the case of listed structures, repairs.

Standing structures are as much a part of the historic environment as 'traditional' below-ground archaeology. Hence the planning guidance and philosophies applied to subsurface deposits and features should be applied in the same manner. As a result, a similar process of appraisal, evaluation, and mitigation (where necessary) should be applied to 'above-ground archaeology' when faced with a development or demolition proposal. This will include buildings and other structures (see, for example, English Heritage 1998 on twentieth-century defences).

PPG15 is complementary to PPG16 in that it concurs with the presumption of preservation *in situ* and the philosophy of replacement 'by record' when preservation *in situ* is not feasible or deemed not to be reasonable. The PPG notes that early consultation with the LPA (and the LGAO) is desirable and that LPAs should expect developers to assess the likely impact of their proposals on the special interest (archaeological significance) of the site or structure in question. Developers should also provide such information or drawings as may be required to understand the significance of a site or structure *before* an application is determined.

When an LGAO's appraisal of an application concludes that a development or demolition proposal has not yet been proved to have no impact on an archaeologically significant standing structure, further information should be requested in advance of determination to inform the decision-making process. This should take the form of a Standing Structure Impact Assessment (as part of an Historic Environment Impact Assessment, when appropriate). Once the relevant information has been presented, an informed decision can be made on the application, with the LGAO (and/or others) advising the LPA on this accordingly. Further mitigation if necessary can be secured through a Section 106 agreement or a negative condition on any planning permission in the usual manner.

Regional and Local Planning Policy

As well as the guidance on archaeology and the historic environment in the two PPGs, archaeological and built environment interests are also safeguarded through the development of relevant policies within Regional Planning Policy Guidance documents and, by LPAs, through Structure Plans and Local Plans.

Regional Planning Policy for the East of England is currently divided between two documents:

- *Regional Planning Guidance Note 6: Regional Planning Guidance for East Anglia to 2016 (RPG6)* (November 2000) covering Cambridgeshire, Peterborough, Norfolk and Suffolk

- *Regional Planning Guidance Note 9: Regional Planning Guidance for the South East (RPG9)* (March 2001) including Bedfordshire, Essex, Hertfordshire, Luton, Southend-on-Sea and Thurrock.

From April 2001, the boundaries for RPG have been brought into line with those for the Government Office for the East of England. In due course *Regional Planning Guidance (RPG14) for the East of England to 2021* will replace RPGs 6 and 9. This is due to be published mid-2004.

In the meantime, the two current RPGs for the region set out strategic aims and objectives for land use and development within a sustainable framework, and provide the regional context for other strategies and programmes, complementing national planning policy guidance.

Objectives within the RPGs include the maintenance and enhancement of the quality of the built environment, including historic settlements, buildings, parks and gardens, open space, conservation areas and archaeological sites. Policies within the RPGs refer to the general management principles for conserving and enhancing the natural, built and historic environment, and the conservation of the region's built and historic environment respectively.

Further information and advice about archaeology and development within the East of England may be obtained from the ALGAOEE contacts listed in Appendix 1.

Future Developments: Planning Policy Statement 15

During 2003 it is anticipated that the Office of the Deputy Prime Minister will be issuing a consultation document on a review of PPGs 15 and 16, leading to the replacement of the PPGs by *Planning Policy Statement 15: Planning for the Historic Environment.*

Planning Policy Statements set out the Government's core policies and principles on different aspects of planning. They should be taken into account by regional planning bodies, strategic and local planning authorities in preparing regional planning guidance, structure plans, unitary plans and local development plans (and subsequently regional spatial strategies and local development frameworks) and will be material to decisions on individual planning applications. Where these policies are not reflected adequately in development plans, or taken into account in relevant development control decisions, the Secretary of State may use his powers of direction to seek changes to the plan and may intervene in planning applications.

PPS15 will in due course replace PPG15 *Planning and the Historic Environment* published in 1994 and PPG16 *Archaeology and Planning* published in 1990. It will be for use by local planning authorities, other public bodies, property owners, developers, amenity bodies and all members of the public with an interest in the conservation of the historic environment.

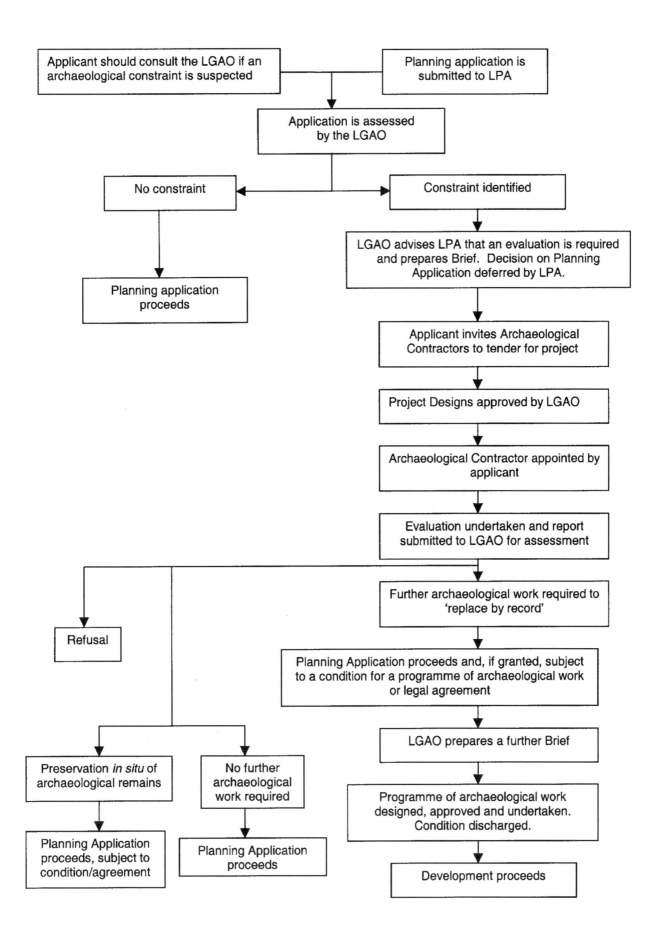

Flow chart illustrating a typical development-led scenario where a planning application is deferred for an archaeological evaluation (right column)

Planning Procedures

The principles of archaeological appraisal, pre-determination evaluation, and mitigation are well integrated into the local planning/development control process, and have been accepted by a wide variety of developers (such as the amenity companies, ecclesiastical authorities, transport and environmental agencies) who work outside the planning system. Developers are increasingly aware of their responsibilities towards the historic environment, and are happy to accommodate best archaeological practice in preserving or recording archaeological remains.

At each stage of the advice process, judgements are made about the value of the archaeological remains in question. The primary intention of this is to secure the preservation of archaeological remains and, where this is not possible, to achieve the creation of a meaningful record that will contribute to knowledge about the past.

Failure to meet the terms and conditions of planning obligations and agreements is a matter of formal enforcement within the Local Planning process. Outside this there are mechanisms for complaint and audit that seek to address shortcomings. These measures, however, cannot usually undo the effects of poor archaeological practice. Disputes occur at the cost of good working relationships between all interested parties, and seldom create a framework for efficient and productive archaeological work.

The LGAO's Appraisal of Planning Applications or Consultations

Archaeological development control advice is based upon a thorough knowledge of the historic environment within the various administrative areas (either Counties, Districts, or Unitary Authorities). The region's Sites and Monuments Records (SMRs), Historic Environment Records (HERs), Urban Archaeological Databases and the National Monuments Record are the principal indices and the primary tools for the initial appraisal of potential development impacts.

Developers and LPAs consult the LGAO on the archaeological implications of development proposals. Developers, their agents and consultants are encouraged to consult the LGAO as soon as possible so that any archaeological interest is identified at an early stage, rather than when a site has been acquired and a planning application submitted.

Consultation with the LGAO prior to the submission of a planning application is the most effective way of protecting the historic environment and managing risks.

The LGAO acts as a specialist adviser to the LPA, but the LPA is responsible for the imposition of conditions, for discharging conditions and, where necessary, for enforcement.

The LGAO's Recommendations to the LPA

The Appraisal by the LGAO will provide information on the archaeological implications of the development and a recommendation to the LPA. This will usually result in one of the following planning decisions:

- refusal of the application

- deferral pending an archaeological evaluation or the assessment of a building

- the imposition of a condition to secure the preservation of archaeological remains *in situ*

- the imposition of a condition to secure the implementation of a programme of archaeological work or building recording

- no archaeological recommendation

If a development site is known to or might possibly include archaeological remains, an Evaluation will be required before the LPA determines the application. This might involve an Archaeological Desk-Based Assessment, field survey, geophysical survey, trial trenching or any combination of these. If important remains are then found to be present and these cannot be preserved *in situ*, the application might be refused or granted subject to a condition for the excavation and recording of the remains.

On other sites of archaeological interest or potential, planning permissions may be granted subject to conditions for programmes of archaeological work. Development control advice provided by archaeologists often culminates in formal planning agreements or conditions, the fulfilment of which requires developing agents to employ archaeological consultants and contractors.

Any programme of work will naturally be informed by the results of any pre-determination evaluation, but if this has not been required the initial works will also be of an investigative nature and may therefore include desk-based work, surveys and/or trial trenching.

Following on from pre-determination evaluation, a further phase (or phases) of archaeological work may be required to complete a programme of archaeological work (and thus discharge the planning condition). This further work might involve, for example, the excavation and recording of defined areas, building recording, or archaeological monitoring and recording (a watching brief).

The fieldwork phase of any project is usually followed by what is generally referred to as Post-Excavation, involving assessment, analysis, report/publication and the preparation and deposition of the project archive. Although these activities take place off-site (and thus the development may have been initiated and possibly even completed while post-excavation work is in progress), they are an integral part of the Programme of Archaeological Work. Any archaeological condition on a planning permission will not be fully discharged until the *full* programme has been completed to the satisfaction of the LGAO and the LPA.

Briefs and Written Schemes of Investigation/ Specifications

When a development proposal raises archaeological issues that require investigation, the LGAO provides a Brief or Specification, an outline of what needs to be done or a more detailed schedule of works respectively. The LGAO should provide this within a reasonable period of time (this will vary according to the complexity of the case).

The LGAO will also be able to advise developers about the appointment of an appropriate Archaeological Consultant or Contractor (for ALGAO best practice in the compilation of lists of contractors, see Campling 1999).

An Archaeological Consultant or Contractor can prepare a Project Design in response to the Brief or Specification. It is advisable for this to be sent to the LGAO for approval before costed proposals are submitted to the client, considering the possible implications of its subsequent rejection by the LGAO. The LGAO should respond in writing to any documents submitted within a reasonable period of time, with comments or approval.

It is expected that all projects will adhere to the project management procedures of *Management of Archaeological Projects* (English Heritage 1991) and that this will be reflected in the structure and content of the Project Design.

The LGAO does not see project costings, nor does he/she give advice on the costs of archaeological projects. This is between a developer and their archaeological contractor(s). A developer may wish to obtain a number of quotations or to employ the services of an archaeological consultant to oversee this process.

The Tendering Process

If a developer (or an archaeological consultant acting on his/her behalf) intends to seek competitive tenders from a number of archaeological contractors then it is best practice for the following procedures to apply:
- the developer should inform all the contractors that they are in a competitive tendering situation and the deadline(s) for submission of Project Designs and costs should be specified;
- contractors should forward their Project Designs to the LGAO for approval as required;
- a developer should only appoint a contractor from those whose Project Designs have been approved by the LGAO;
- a developer should seek to appoint a contractor who will provide a high-quality service, not just the lowest price.

It is very important to note that the resources required for the post-excavation phase of any project cannot be predicted with certainty in advance, although indicative costs for assessment, analysis, report, publication and the deposition of the archive for an small evaluation project or watching brief may reasonably be estimated at the same time as the costs of fieldwork.

For excavation projects, archaeological contractors and consultants should advise their potential clients that the costs of post-excavation work can only be determined after the excavation has been completed and its results assessed.

The LGAO may be able to provide information (usually a list) about archaeological contractors and consultants working in the region.

The Institute of Field Archaeologists (IFA) publishes a directory of its members and Registered Archaeological Organisations (RAOs). Archaeological contractors and consultants may employ staff who are Members (MIFA), Associates (AIFA) or Practitioners (PIFA) of the IFA and who, as individuals, carry out archaeological work in accordance with the Institute's *Code of Conduct*. Work by RAOs is only carried out by, or under the responsibility of, a suitably experienced corporate member (MIFA) with appropriate Areas of Competence. The RAO scheme does not itself define detailed standards for best practice, but it seeks to provide a general control against which adherence to professional standards can be judged.

The Standing Conference of Archaeological Unit Managers has published guidance on competitive tendering in archaeology (1996).

The Institute of Field Archaeologists has published a code of practice for the regulation of contractual arrangements in field archaeology (1997b) and draft principles of conduct for archaeologists involved in commercial archaeological work (1998).

Regional Standards

The *Regional Standards* have been ordered thematically, primarily because many of the topics addressed are applicable to more than one form of archaeological fieldwork, including development-led projects, research projects and amateur (non-vocational) activities. Where appropriate, project documents (development-led or not) may usefully refer to the relevant sections of the *Standards*. For example, an archaeological evaluation in a rural context prior to the determination of a planning application might find some or all of the following sections especially relevant:

General Requirements (1.1 to 1.16)

Desk-Based Research (2.1 to 2.5)

Fieldwalking (3.1 to 3.7)

Metal-detecting (3.8 to 3.15)

Geophysical surveys (3.20 to 3.21)

Intrusive Methodologies (4.1 to 4.13)

Evaluation (4.14 to 4.18)

Finds and conservation (7.1 to 7.5)

Archaeological Science (8)

Reports (9.1 to 9.18, 9.25 to 9.32)

Publication (10)

Archives (11)

Project Monitoring (12)

and reference to these sections of the *Standards* may be included, where appropriate, in the project Brief or Project Design.

1. General Requirements

1.1 It is advisable for Project Designs/Method Statements/Written Schemes prepared by archaeological contractors/consultants to be submitted to the LGAO (as adviser to the LPA) and approved in writing by the LGAO *before* proposals or estimates of costs or quotations are provided to the potential client. This is best practice in line with the Institute of Field Archaeologists' guidance (1997b), although it is recognised that practice across the region varies. The requirements of the LGAO's Brief regarding submission of documents must be adhered to.

1.2 Project Designs will be rejected if it is determined that they:

- are insufficiently documented
- do not meet the requirements specified in the Brief or Specification
- fail to demonstrate the Archaeological Contractor's competence and ability to undertake the project in accordance with this *Regional Standards* document.

In the event of a Project Design being rejected by the LGAO the archaeological contractor or consultant will be informed of the reason(s).

1.3 The LGAO may refer to appropriate research objectives in the Brief or Specification, or the archaeological contractor or consultant will be expected to consider what these might be. Either way, the Project Design must provide a clear statement of the project's aims and objectives within the context of national and regional research frameworks, especially Glazebrook 1997 and Brown and Glazebrook 2000.

1.4 All projects must be undertaken in accordance with relevant professional standards. IFA Membership and adherence to IFA's Codes of Conduct (IFA 1997a, 1997b) and formally adopted by-laws, guidelines and other relevant codes, standards and guidance documents are regarded as baseline standards and yardsticks of competence and good operating practice. Archaeologists working on a project should not attempt tasks outside their Areas of Competence.

1.5 Archaeological contractors/consultants are advised, as a matter of course during the preparation of Project Designs, to inspect the site in question and undertake sufficient background research to familiarise themselves with the archaeology of the site and its environs.

1.6 Where required by the LGAO in the Brief or Specification, archaeological projects will be managed following the guidance in English Heritage's *Management of Archaeological Projects* (1991) (often referred to as MAP2 and *cf* English Heritage n.d.).

1.7 Project Designs must provide details of:

- the qualifications and relevant experience of the Project Manager, project team, key personnel, subcontractors and specialists
- a timetable of work
- the arrangements to provide the LGAO with the required advance notice of the start of work and opportunities for monitoring. No fieldwork should be carried out with the required prior notification of the LGAO.

1.8 The Project Manager and any other supervisory staff will ensure that all members of the archaeological team are appropriately informed as to the projects' methodologies and objectives.

1.9 Professional archaeologists in the employ of the archaeological contractor must undertake all work being undertaken to meet the requirements of the Brief or Specification. Any *additional* work being undertaken by students or volunteer staff must be specified.

1.10 All archaeological work will pay due regard to Health and Safety considerations. Guidance on Health and Safety may be found in Standing Conference of Archaeological Unit Managers 1997. Contractors must carry out Risk

Assessments for all activities, including arrangements for Project Monitoring by the LGAO.

1.11 It is the responsibility of the archaeological contractor/consultant to ensure that adequate resources have been made available by the client to complete the programme of archaeological work set out in the Project Design and to fulfill the Brief or Specification.

1.12 Any subsequent variations by an archaeological contractor/consultant from an approved Project Design must be agreed with the LGAO prior to implementation.

1.13 Briefs or Specifications issued by an LGAO are usually valid for a specified period from the date of issue. After that time, they may need to be revised to take account of new discoveries, changes in policy or the introduction of new working practices or techniques.

1.14 Project Designs where required will include a provisional programme for the Assessment and Analysis phases of the project (where appropriate), following MAP2. The Analysis and Publication Programme will be reviewed at the Assessment stage.

1.15 For any project, all numbering and coding must be compatible with the relevant Sites and Monuments Record or Historic Environment Record. The relevant SMR/HER Officer upon request usually issues site numbers and, where appropriate, parish codes and starting context numbers. It is essential that archaeological contractors/consultants should obtain advice *before* numbers and codes are allocated on site.

1.16 All project records must be clearly marked with the relevant County Number, civil parish name or code, site name and date (following local requirements).

2. Desk-Based Research

Desk-based research is undertaken to determine, as far as is reasonably possible from existing records, the nature of the archaeological resource within a specified area.

2.1 Archaeological Desk-Based Assessments (ADBA) must be prepared following the *Standard and Guidance for Archaeological Desk-Based Assessments* (Institute of Field Archaeologists 1999a). It is advisable to consult the LGAO to define requirements and, if necessary, submit a Project Design.

2.2 An ADBA will also make full and effective use of existing information to establish the archaeological significance and potential of the defined area, drawing upon some or all of the following sources:

- a report of a site visit (compulsory)
- the Sites and Monuments Record or Historic Environment Record (compulsory)
- available historic maps (compulsory)
- geological maps
- Ordnance Survey maps of the site and its environs
- tithe apportionment, enclosure and parish maps
- estate maps
- documentary and cartographic collections held by the relevant record office

desk-based research

- Local Studies libraries
- historical documents held in other record offices, local museums, libraries or other archives
- enrolled deeds
- archaeological and historical books and journals
- unpublished research reports and archives held by relevant museums, local societies and archaeological contractors and consultants
- all sources of aerial photography, including the National Monuments Record and the Cambridge University Collection of Aerial Photographs (see below)
- borehole and trial pit data
- geophysical and/or geotechnical data.

2.3 Where an ADBA is required, staff with experience in the preparation of such reports will be used. This must identify and plot:

- all areas of known and potential archaeological significance within the defined area;
- all areas where activities may have destroyed or truncated archaeological remains;
- any areas of known or potential ground contamination;
- the scale and nature of the development proposal if known;
- relevant constraints (*e.g.* Scheduled Ancient Monuments, Conservation Areas and Listed Buildings). Where non-archaeological constraints are identified (*e.g.* Sites of Special Scientific Interest, sites of wildlife interest, protected species, Tree Preservation Orders, Countryside Stewardship Schemes, Environmentally Sensitive Areas), it is helpful if these are included;
- geology, soils, drainage, anticipated preservation conditions and variables affecting preservation of biological remains and organic artefacts;
- any previous investigations in Archaeological Science at the site or immediately adjacent to it (*cf* 8. below).

2.4 Where an accurate plot of cropmarks is required, this will usually be prepared at a scale of 1:2500, or 1:10,000 for larger relatively uncomplicated areas. In some parts of the region, English Heritage's *National Mapping Programme* (NMP) has been completed and in other areas it is in progress. Where NMP data is available, this must be consulted.

2.5 All sources consulted must be listed.

3. Non-Intrusive Surveys

Field surveys of various kinds provide non-intrusive, non-destructive and cost-effective ways of collecting archaeological data. Fieldwalking and metal-detecting can recover information from artefacts on the surface of or within the ploughsoil or topsoil, whilst geophysical surveys can locate buried archaeological structures and features.

The first two sub-sections below (3.1 to 3.15) refer to extensive surveys undertaken in order to acquire a representative sample of artefact type and size classes present, to investigate locations and areas of occupation, to assess the effects of tillage on artefact distributions and to define areas for possible further archaeological investigation.

Where, for other reasons, intensive transects or gridded surface collection is required, this will be dealt with in the Project Brief or Specification.

On large or complex sites, a phased programme of evaluation or excavation may be adopted. Where field survey or geophysical survey needs to be followed by trial trenching or excavation, the trenching or excavation strategy will be determined once the survey results have been assessed.

Fieldwalking

3.1 Fieldwalking may only be carried out in suitable weather and light conditions, after appropriate cultivation, weathering and washing of the field surface. The surface conditions at the time of survey must be fully documented in the report, along with other variables (*e.g.* weather, light, obstructions, topography, collector *etc*), and the impact of these variables on the recovery of data should be assessed.

3.2 Staff who fieldwalk must have experience of artefact recognition.

3.3 The survey grid will be established by measured survey technique. In all cases work must be related to fixed points, plotted and fully documented so that, if necessary, the precise locations of those surveys can be accurately re-established. It may be a requirement for fieldwork transects to be tied in to and aligned on the national grid. In other cases, grids may be aligned on appropriate landscape features.

3.4 Transects for fieldwalking should be at 20 metre intervals, unless otherwise specified. Search/collection units of specified length will be employed to locate concentrations of artefacts.

3.5 The fieldwalkers will generally observe a 2 metre wide strip along each transect, thereby examining a minimum 10% sample of the field surface.

3.6 Finds from each collection unit must be individually bagged, numbered, labelled and marked by context, and recorded on appropriate pro forma Fieldwalking Recording Sheets.

3.7 Where large amounts of *e.g.* post-medieval brick or tile fragments or burnt flints are not collected, the presence of this material must be recorded.

Metal-detecting

Systematic metal-detecting recovers a range of archaeological objects that is complementary to those classes of artefacts usually found by fieldwalking, *i.e.* flints, pottery and building materials. A metal-detector survey may retrieve metal artefacts from the Bronze Age onwards and coins from the Iron Age onwards. Some sites such as dispersed hoards of metalwork or coins and Anglo-Saxon inhumation cemeteries are more likely to be located by metal-detecting than by any other technique.

3.8 The recovery of archaeological objects located by metal-detector is an activity which, for the purposes of field survey, is to be restricted to the ploughsoil. In the event that an object or group of objects is located below ploughsoil depth, these must initially be left *in situ* while arrangements are made for their recovery under controlled excavation conditions.

3.9 Metal-detecting must be undertaken in appropriate conditions. Low stubble is often ideal.

3.10 Experienced and competent operators in the employ of the archaeological contractor, using reliable and well-maintained equipment, may only carry out metal-detecting as a separate activity from fieldwalking.

3.11 The strategy for metal-detecting (transects, collection units *etc*) is broadly the same as that used for fieldwalking. The transects may be parallel to the fieldwalking transects if units are being searched by fieldwalkers and metal-detectorists simultaneously.

3.12 It is generally acceptable to discriminate against iron objects.

3.13 It is generally acceptable to discard items of no archaeological significance. However, when the date and function of an object is unknown or uncertain it must be retained for examination by finds staff and/or relevant specialists.

3.14 A pro forma recording sheet will include details of conditions, the equipment used, discriminator level, operator *etc*, and a general comment about any discarded material.

3.15 All Treasure and finds of potential Treasure must be dealt with in accordance with the *Treasure Act* 1996 and its Code of Practice.

Earthwork surveys

For defined levels of recording for archaeological surveys, see Royal Commission on the Historical Monuments of England 1999.

3.16 Staff with appropriate survey and interpretative experience must be used in order to ensure uniformity of results.

3.17 Survey may be undertaken using instrumental and/or graphic methods, depending on the topography and the experience of staff. Whichever is employed, the survey methodology and the format of the interpretative drawings must be agreed with the LGAO before commencement.

3.18 The preferred method will be specified in the Brief, but it may include:

- digital data, where required, in a format to be agreed with the LGAO

- drawings on a film base at a scale of 1:1000, or 1:500 if greater detail is required

- at least two National Grid intersections

- earthwork features depicted by hachures

- sufficient detail of the adjacent topography so that the survey can be easily related to present-day landscape features

- profiles across any earthworks

- an analytical report presented as an integral part of the survey, with description and interpretation referenced by letters or numbers to the plan.

Aerial photographic surveys

Aerial photographic survey can be an important component of archaeological survey and may provide a level of detail that cannot be achieved by other means. Where ground conditions are favourable, aerial survey can record evidence of geological disturbances, the periglacial landscape, soil erosion and accumulation, and cut or embanked features.

3.19 All survey must be undertaken in accordance with the Institute of Field Archaeologists' Technical Paper 12, *Uses of Aerial Photography in Archaeological Evaluations* (Palmer and Cox 1993) and the Council for British Archaeology's *Aerial Archaeology Guidance Note* (1995).

Geophysical surveys

Non-intrusive geophysical surveys may provide a great deal of information about the extent and nature of below-ground structures and subsoil features. They are often therefore ideal (and cost-effective) techniques for site evaluation. The three main techniques are magnetometry (fluxgate gradiometer), magnetic susceptibility and resistivity. Careful consideration must be given to obtaining specialist advice, the appointment of an appropriate contractor, and the selection of the most suitable and effective technique taking into account the individual circumstances of each site. The results from test-pits or boreholes, if available, may assist with this. See also 8.3-8.6 below.

3.20 All survey must be undertaken in accordance with *The Use of Geophysical Techniques in Archaeological Evaluation* (Gaffney, Gater and Ovenden 2002) and *Geophysical survey in Archaeological Field Evaluation* (David 1995).

3.21 For best practice in the creation and use of digital geophysical data, see Schmidt 2001.

4. Intrusive Methodologies

General requirements

4.1 Project Designs must include details of:

- the proposed locations and extent of trial trenches or excavation areas (with scale plans)

- the excavation and recording strategy

- the arrangements for palaeoenvironmental assessment and analysis (*cf* 8.16-8.19 below)

- the arrangements to provide the LGAO with the required advance notice of the start of work and opportunities for monitoring

- the levels of intervention proposed in the excavation by hand of various types of contexts that may be encountered. In the case of Evaluations, where the objective is to define remains rather than totally remove them, investigation should not be at the expense of any structures, deposits, features or finds which might reasonably be considered to merit preservation *in situ*. It is important, however, that sufficient work is done to allow the resolution of the principal aims and objectives of the project

- provision for the identification of artefacts

- site security with particular reference to finds and records

- conservation facilities and expertise, both for on-site 'first aid' for finds and as part of the post-excavation process

- specialists who might be required to advise or report on archaeological science or other aspects of the investigation

- report strategy

- archive strategy.

4.2 A mechanical excavator working under close and constant archaeological supervision may usually remove all undifferentiated topsoil or overburden of recent origin in spits down to the first significant archaeological horizon. A mechanical excavator with a wide ditching bucket with teeth removed will usually be used for this. In some instances, topsoil layers may themselves require excavation, in which case this will be specified in the Brief. Any machine excavation of archaeological deposits (*e.g.* bulk deposits of little archaeological or environmental potential) may only be undertaken with the prior agreement of the LGAO.

4.3 Provision must be made for the cleaning by hand of the faces of trenches and, where appropriate, the machined surface.

4.4 Unless specified otherwise in the Brief, the areas indicated on the scale plans accompanying a Project Design will be excavated to natural, thereby recovering a complete sequence of ground plans of any archaeological deposits or features within those areas. However, investigation should not be at the expense of any structures, deposits, features or finds which might reasonably be considered to merit preservation *in situ* (*cf* 4.1).

4.5 Buried soils and/or specific contexts will be sampled and sieved or bulk-sieved in order to maximise the retrieval of artefacts and environmental evidence from significant deposits (*cf* 8.12 below).

4.6 Provision will be made, where appropriate, for scientific dating and analysis, including C14, dendrochronological and archaeomagnetic dating (*cf* 8.7-8.10 below).

4.7 Where deposits are encountered with the potential for providing scientific dating evidence, palaeoenvironmental evidence or other information related to archaeological science (see section 8 below), the advice of the LGAO and English Heritage's Regional Advisor for Archaeological Science must be obtained. An appropriate excavation and sampling strategy will be agreed and included in the Project Design.

4.8 Trenches or excavation areas must not be backfilled without the prior approval of the LGAO unless this is necessary for safety reasons.

4.9 Where obstructions are encountered unexpectedly, minor variations to trench/area layout may usually be made without consulting the LGAO. However, any substantive changes to the agreed strategy must be agreed with the LGAO before implementation.

4.10 Any human remains that are encountered unexpectedly must initially be left *in situ*, covered and protected (*cf* 8.20-8.25 below). If removal is necessary, this must comply with the relevant Home Office regulations, Section 25 of the Burial Act 1857, the Disused Burial Grounds (Amendment) Act 1981 (where appropriate) and the relevant environmental health regulations.

4.11 Archaeological contractors will employ standardised and documented recording methods, generally utilising pro forma recording sheets. Copies of these must be sent to the LGAO for approval.

4.12 All archaeological contexts and artefacts exposed or examined must be adequately surveyed, sampled, cleaned, planned, excavated and *replaced by record* on appropriate pro forma context, finds and sample sheets, by the production of plans, sections and elevations at appropriate scales and by black and white and colour photographic record.

4.13 An on-site index of plans and sections and other on-site records must be maintained, and eventually included in the project archive.

Evaluation

This is an intrusive methodology **which may be** required prior to the determination of a planning application, with the aim of informing the decision-making process on the best course of action for an archaeological deposit sequence to be affected by a proposed development programme.

4.14 Project Designs must confirm that the aim of the work is to create a full characterisation of the archaeological sequence and a model of the deposit history. The methodology to be used must be articulated and the sources to be consulted listed.

4.15 Evaluation trial-trenching will recover as much information as possible on the extent, date, phasing, character, function, status and significance of the site. The states of preservation of archaeological features or deposits within the area indicated must be determined.

4.16 Evaluation trial-trenching will normally examine an appropriate sample (often expressed as a % of the area of the proposed development site) as required by the Brief or Specification (*cf* Hey and Lacey 2001). The area of the *base* of a battered or stepped trench will usually be the figure used to determine if the sample has been achieved. In urban areas, smaller samples may sometimes be specified taking into account the particular circumstances on a site-by-site basis. Where the sample size is not stipulated in the Brief, a rationale for the sampling method must be provided based on knowledge and understanding of the surrounding archaeological resource.

4.17 Exceptionally, and only with the prior approval of the LGAO, the mechanical removal of archaeological deposits may be permitted.

4.18 An archive and client report must be produced. In some instances, publication of the evaluation results may be required if no further work is undertaken and if the results of the evaluation warrant dissemination of a synthesis of the results in an appropriate journal.

Excavation

An Excavation may be required where it has been decided that any archaeological remains do not warrant physical preservation *in situ*, and that an acceptable mitigation strategy is for these to be excavated archaeologically, replaced by record, assessed, analysed, archived and a synthesis of the results disseminated. For standards and guidance see also Institute of Field Archaeologists 1999d.

4.19 Excavation Projects will recover as much information as possible on the origins, date, development, phasing, spatial organisation, character, function, status, significance and the nature of social, economic and industrial activities on the site.

4.20 Excavation Projects will examine, excavate and replace by record all archaeological features, deposits and structures within the area indicated and to the agreed depth, assess their potential for analysis, undertake an agreed programme of analysis, produce a report (9 below), archive (11 below), and publication (10 below).

4.21 Archaeological contractors must provide sufficient, secure and separate accommodation for site records, and for finds processing and finds storage if these activities take place on site.

4.22 Provision of access is an important tenet of archaeological excavation, and a Brief may include encouragement to bring the circumstances, results, analysis and interpretation of archaeological work before the general public (open days, viewing platforms, site tours, on-site provision of information and publicity (where allowed) in the local and national media). Opportunities should also be provided, where practicable, for local amateur archaeological groups to participate. This, it must be stressed, should in no way replace any aspect of the formal costed works to meet the requirements of the Brief or Specification.

Archaeological Monitoring (or Watching Brief)

Archaeological Monitoring and Recording (or a Watching Brief) means that an archaeologist must be present throughout or during certain specified phases of the development to record any features exposed or any archaeological finds.

In the event of the discovery of unanticipated remains of national importance, discussions will take place (which might include the developer, the LGAO, the LPA and English Heritage) on how these might be preserved *in situ* or recorded.

For standards and guidance see also Institute of Field Archaeologists 1999c.

4.23 During Archaeological Monitoring and Recording, provision must be made for an archaeologist(s) to be present during specified times and/or activities including, where required:

- all areas of below-ground disturbance, including excavations, foundation trenches, service trenches, drains and soakaways

- above-ground remains when the development affects a building of historic importance

- pipelines and cable trenches.

4.24 Monitoring will be undertaken at the level or intensity indicated in the Brief or Specification. This may involve intensive monitoring (*i.e.* continuous presence during activities), regular monitoring visits or occasional monitoring (a programme of planned visits to coincide with relevant activities).

4.25 The archaeological contractor must be in full control of machining activity on the site.

4.26 Where required, all topsoil or spoil must be scanned carefully by eye and surveyed by metal-detector during its removal.

4.27 Monitoring and Recording of a standing structure is a particularly useful approach for small-scale, focussed developments and repair proposals involving minimal opening up of discrete areas of a structure. It will generally include, as a minimum:

- monitoring of fabric intervention to structure

- recording by photography and scale drawing of fabric revealed, altered or removed.

5. Urban Archaeology
by Andy Hutcheson

The defining difference between an urban and any other sort of archaeological site is, of course, the past intensity of use. A less interpretatively-loaded description of such a situation could be 'intensively stratified archaeological areas'. Regardless of the nuances of various definitions, the reality is that these stratified archaeological situations require a specific set of approaches and skills. A Project Design for a stratified site must therefore articulate a methodology appropriate to the nature of the archaeological deposits to be investigated and the environment in which the work will take place.

intensive stratification

There is a useful body of literature on methodological approaches to the archaeology of towns, notably Harris' work on understanding stratigraphy (1975, 1979, 1984 and 1993), Carver (1987; 1990), the Museum of London's archaeological site manuals (Spence 1990; 1994), the proceedings of the *Interpreting Stratigraphy* conferences (Steane 1992, Barber 1993, Shepherd 1995, Roskams 1998; 2000); Chadwick 1997, Thorpe 1998 and Roskams 2001.

Recording (evaluation and excavation)

Recording of the contextual situation and the relationships between deposits is of primary importance in any archaeological investigation. The major difference in an urban environment is that the deposit sequence will usually be more complex. There are a number of methodological tools that can be applied to the recording of this complexity. Most important of these is the record made of the relative position of a defined context in relation to the rest of the sequence through the use of a stratigraphic matrix. The construction and subsequent analysis of a matrix, both on site and in post-excavation, will greatly enhance the interpretative value of the investigation and will allow any future researcher to approach the primary site record more easily.

Also of great value to both understanding the sequence on site and creating an interpretable archive is a single context planning methodology. Linking of these two recording methods, along with the text record, results in a powerful interpretative tool for analysis of any archaeological deposit sequence. In many cases it may be appropriate to carry this further and utilise information technology to assist in the process of understanding.

Evaluation sampling

Given the nature of the urban environment and the potential necessity for deep trenches, evaluation will be a relatively more costly exercise in towns. The object of evaluation is to characterise the archaeological sequence and its present and future research value. In order to accomplish this the entire sequence present within a proposed development area will need to be modelled. This may require a significant sample of the site and a detailed synthesis of the results of evaluation with other information held on the location in archaeological databases, documents and maps.

Preservation *in situ*

The aim of much evaluation in the urban context is to decide on the best course of action for an archaeological deposit sequence affected by a proposed development programme. A range of possible solutions can be formulated to meet the challenge of reconciling the survival of a particular archaeological resource with the need for development. Very often the choice of solution will rest on whether the development scheme can be built on top of the archaeological remains. Piling and minimally intrusive foundation designs will be chosen for situations where it can be demonstrated that the remains can be effectively preserved through such an approach. In cases where there are anaerobic conditions resulting in organic preservation, evaluation must attempt to answer difficult questions such as:

- will the local environment be affected?

- how can the environment be monitored throughout the life of the building?

- what will be the affect of this development on the surrounding archaeological resource?

Approaches to evaluation that attempt to minimise on-site costs through stepping of the trenches can defeat the purpose of preservation. Destruction of part of the sequence without record is not an acceptable methodology, given the logic of the evaluation exercise. Shoring of deeply stratified evaluation trenches is usually the most effective way of characterising the resource whilst minimising its destruction.

There is presently a small but growing body of literature relating to the preservation of archaeological sites *in situ* (see Corfield *et al.* 1996).

5.1 All archaeological investigations of stratified deposit sequences will construct an ongoing matrix of the relationships between the contexts defined within the trench.

5.2 A single context planning methodology will normally be used to ensure both a greater understanding of the site sequence by the archaeologists carrying out the investigation but also so that sequential interpretations can be reproduced.

5.3 Project Designs must confirm that the aim of the work is to create a full characterisation of the archaeological sequence and a model of the deposit history. The methodology to be used must be articulated and the sources to be consulted discussed. Where the sample size is not stipulated in the Brief, a rationale for the sampling method must be provided based on knowledge and understanding of the surrounding archaeological resource.

5.4 Project Designs must confirm that where a sequence in excess of 1.2m in depth is expected, provision for the required methodology (normally trench shoring) has been made.

5.5 Project Designs must articulate the range of preservation considerations to be investigated and reported on during the evaluation. In cases where organic preservation in anaerobic conditions is likely, an appropriate range of scientific measurements and environmental tests should be built into the Project Design and analysed for the report (*e.g.* pH and redox) as well as an assessment of organic preservation.

5.6 Excavation areas will generally be stipulated in the brief. The stipulated area does not include steps for edge protection and a methodology for providing safe excavation sides must be articulated in the Project Design.

6. Standing Structures
by Jonathan Smith

There is a variety of practice across the region with regard to the assessment and recording of standing structures. In some authorities, the LGAO may only advise on non-listed structures, while in others the LPA's Conservation Officers may deal with above-ground buildings archaeology.

6.1 Work must be undertaken in accordance with the guidance contained in the following documents:

- *Recording Historic Buildings; A Descriptive Specification* (3rd edition) (Royal Commission on the Historical Monuments of England 1996)

- *Analysis and recording for the conservation and control of works to historic buildings* (Association of County Archaeological Officers 1997)

- *Standard and Guidance for the Archaeological Investigation and Recording of Standing Buildings or Structures* (Institute of Field Archaeologists 1999e).

6.2 An archaeological contractor who is a suitably qualified buildings archaeologist, conservation architect, or art historian will carry out all assessments and fieldwork. The LGAO will be able to advise on the appointment of an appropriate contractor.

6.3 Where a Standing Structure Impact Assessment is required, this will usually include, as a minimum, an Archaeological Desk-Based Assessment, an outline photographic survey, measured plans, elevations, or other surveys representing the existing structure, drawings in plan and elevation indicating the proposed development, and a complete planning history of the site. This may be required before an application is determined, in cases where the information has not already been included with an application. In the case of demolition proposals, the LGAO may wish to request a fuller level of recording at this stage when the structure has potential for archaeological significance.

6.4 The aims and objectives of a programme of work involving building recording will generally be to:

- compile a comprehensive and high quality record of the structures subject to the development/demolition proposal

- provide a comprehensive review of the local and regional historical context of the structures recorded by the project in the resultant analytical report. This must be adequately detailed to place the findings of the recording in their context and to be able to inform conservation decisions and the subsequent management of the structures

- produce a high quality, fully integrated archive suitable for long-term deposition in order to replace by record the structures in their form prior to conversion, alteration, demolition or repair.

6.5 The contractor must complete the required surveys and submit the report *prior to the commencement of development or demolition* of the structures subject to the application. Further recording may be required of interventions into the fabric of the original structure in the case of alteration, conversion, and/or repair of the structure in question. This, if justified (particularly so with Listed Buildings and Scheduled Ancient Monuments), will complete the archive and facilitate its use as a future conservation and management tool for the structure.

7. Finds and Conservation
see also 8.26-8.35 below

7.1 All finds work must be to accepted professional standards, and the *Standard and Guidance for the collection, documentation, conservation and research of archaeological materials* (Institute of Field Archaeologists 2001) adhered to.

7.2 Finds must be processed as soon as possible after recovery so that staff in the field can receive feedback and spot-dating of archaeological deposits being excavated.

7.3 During the assessment of metal finds, the advice of a professional conservator must be sought on conservation and x-ray requirements. All metal objects (except those of lead) must be x-rayed, and the x-rays included in the site archive as an integral component of the finds records (*cf* 8.29 below).

7.4 No sampling or disposal of cultural material from an evaluation or excavation may take place without prior approval by the LGAO and the intended place of deposition of the project archive.

7.5 All Treasure and finds of potential Treasure must be dealt with in accordance with the *Treasure Act* 1996 and its Code of Practice.

`have you washed those pots yet?'

8. Archaeological Science
by Peter Murphy

To separate 'Archaeological Science' from 'Field Archaeology' is of course artificial (for there are wide areas of overlap) but, for practical reasons and to avoid duplication, it is necessary in this document. Archaeological Science is here taken to include:

- geophysics
- scientific dating
- geoarchaeology and soil science
- analysis of botanical and faunal remains
- analysis of human remains
- artefact conservation and investigative analysis
- analysis of technological residues, ceramics, glass and stone.

This section applies equally to both evaluations and excavations, ranging from pre-determination evaluations through to evaluations and excavations secured by conditions. Evaluations differ widely in scope, scale and objectives. Small-scale initial pre-determination evaluations are usually intended to establish whether any archaeology is present at all and in this case Archaeological Science will often not be applicable. For all subsequent fieldwork it certainly is.

Procedures for desk-based studies, evaluation and excavation at coastal managed realignment schemes are to be found in Trow and Murphy (forthcoming). Most of these procedures are also applicable at other types of site where deep sediment sequences occur.

Specialists

Except in the field of artefact conservation, there are currently no professional accreditation schemes. Elsewhere, an objective criterion of competence is the ability of specialists to demonstrate that they have access to adequate laboratory facilities, including reference collections where needed. The phrase 'recognised specialist' is used below as a neutral, non-prescriptive term.

8.1 Specialists in archaeological science will be named in Project Designs and their competence to undertake investigations must be demonstrated. It is reasonable to expect a qualification, record of publication or training/mentoring by an experienced specialist.

8.2 There must be agreement in writing between the archaeological contractor/consultant and specialists on timetables and deadlines for all stages of work.

Geophysical prospection

8.3 The standards presented in *Geophysical Survey in Archaeological Field Evaluations* (David 1995) represent best practice.

8.4 Where a programme of geophysical survey is required, a recognised specialist in the techniques involved must be employed.

8.5 For most substrates, magnetometer survey is often the preferred technique in the first instance, using a fluxgate gradiometer with digital data storage and transfer facility.

8.6 If other techniques are to be employed, the geophysicist must provide a statement explaining the reasons for their use. The choice and deployment of techniques must be agreed with the LGAO in the light of this and after initial assessment of site conditions.

Scientific dating

As a guide to the potential usage of scientific dating, it has already been applied during evaluation in the East of England in the following circumstances:

- radiocarbon dating of wooden structures which were not dated artefactually or stratigraphically

- radiocarbon dating of organic sediment sequences believed to be contemporary with adjacent archaeological sites

- OSL (Optically Stimulated Luminescence) dating of colluvial sediments overlying cut archaeological features, undertaken to help define the appropriate depth of machining during subsequent excavation.

8.7 During field evaluation, samples will be taken for scientific dating in defined and specific circumstances, subject to time constraints. This applies where dating by artefacts is insecure or absent and where dating is necessary for development of the Project Design or Specification for subsequent work.

8.8 Samples for dating must be submitted to the laboratory promptly, following both evaluation and excavation. Prior agreement will be made with the laboratory on turn-around time and report production, so as to ensure that results are available to aid development of specifications for subsequent mitigation strategies, or for excavation report production.

8.9 During excavation projects, samples must be collected for radiocarbon, dendrochronology, luminescence, archaeomagnetism (and/or other techniques as appropriate) following the outline strategy presented in the Project Design/Specification. A detailed and cost-effective strategy for scientific dating will be prepared in consultation with appropriate specialists.

8.10 Sampling for dendrochronology must follow procedures presented in *Dendrochonology: guidelines on producing and interpreting dendrochronological dates* (Hillam 1998).

Geoarchaeology

8.11 Procedures and techniques presented in *Guidelines for carrying out Assessments in Geoarchaeology* (Canti 1996) should be followed.

8.12 Buried soils and sediment sequences must be inspected and recorded on site at both the evaluation and excavation stage by a recognised geoarchaeologist. Field inspection can provide sufficient data for understanding site formation processes, thereby avoiding the collection and processing of redundant samples.

bulk sieving

8.13 Samples for laboratory assessment and analysis will be collected where appropriate, following discussion with the LGAO.

8.14 Samples will be processed as deemed necessary by the specialist, particularly where storage of unprocessed samples is thought likely to result in deterioration. Appropriate assessment must be undertaken. Where preservation *in situ* is a viable option, consideration should be given to the possible effects of compression on the physical integrity of the site and to any hydrological impacts of development.

8.15 During excavation, samples will be collected for analysis of chemistry, magnetic susceptibility, particle size, micromorphology and/or other techniques as appropriate, following the outline strategy presented in the Project Design/Specification, and in consultation with the geoarchaeologist.

Botanical and faunal remains

8.16 During evaluation, deposits will be sampled for retrieval and assessment of the preservation conditions and potential for analysis of biological remains. The sampling strategy must include a reasoned justification for selection of deposits for sampling, and will be developed in collaboration with a recognised bioarchaeologist.

8.17 Sampling methods for macrofossils (e.g. shells, seeds) and microfossils (*e.g.* pollen, foraminiferans) must follow the document *Environmental Archaeology. A guide to the theory and practice of methods, from sampling and recovery to post-excavation* (English Heritage 2002).

8.18 Bulk samples and samples taken for coarse-mesh sieving from dry deposits must be processed at the time of the fieldwork wherever possible, partly to permit variation of sampling strategies if necessary, but also because processing a backlog of samples at a later stage can cause delays. Sampling strategies for wooden structures must follow the methodologies presented in Brunning 1996.

8.19 Biological samples from both evaluations and excavations must be assessed by recognised bioarchaeologists for evidence of site formation and taphonomy. Processing of all soil samples collected for biological assessment, or sub-samples of them, should be completed, except where deposits prove to be undatable. The preservation, state, density and significance of material retrieved must be assessed. Special consideration should be given to any evidence for recent changes in preservation conditions that may have been caused by alterations in the site environment. Unprocessed sub-samples must be stored in conditions specified by the appropriate specialists. Animal bone assemblages, or sub-samples of them, must be assessed by a recognised specialist. Following assessment, appropriate samples of biological materials must be analysed.

Human remains

8.20 At the evaluation stage, lifting of human skeletal remains must be kept to the minimum that is compatible with an adequate evaluation.

8.21 At sites known in advance to be cemeteries, provision must be made for site inspection by a recognised specialist.

8.22 Excavators must be aware of, and comply with, the relevant legislation and any Home Office and local environmental health concerns. Further guidance is provided in *Church Archaeology: its care and management* (Council for the Care of Churches 1999).

8.23 Assessment of human remains will be based partly on *in situ* observation, but where skeletal remains have been lifted, a recognised specialist must undertake assessment.

8.24 During excavation, burials must be recorded *in situ* and subsequently lifted, washed in water (without any additives), marked and packed to standards compatible with *Excavation and post-excavation treatment of cremated and inhumed human remains* (McKinley and Roberts 1993). Site inspection by a recognised specialist is desirable in the case of isolated non-complex burials, and necessary for cemeteries.

8.25 Proposals for the final placing of human remains following study and analysis will be required in the Project Design/Specification. Further guidance is provided in *Church Archaeology: its care and management* (Council for the Care of Churches 1999).

Artefact conservation and investigative analysis

8.26 All finds visible or located by other means (such as metal-detecting) during evaluation and excavation must be collected and processed, unless variations in this principle are agreed with the LGAO.

8.27 Provision must be made, where appropriate, for the regular transfer of finds from a site to the conservation laboratory.

8.28 Finds must be appropriately packaged and stored under optimum conditions, as detailed in *First Aid for Finds* (Watkinson and Neal 1998).

8.29 Assessment must include x-radiography of all metal objects (after initial screening to exclude obviously recent debris) except those of lead (*cf* 7.3 above). A rapid scan of all excavated material must be undertaken by conservators and finds researchers in collaboration. Material considered vulnerable will be selected for stabilisation after specialist recording. Where intervention is necessary, consideration should be given to possible investigative procedures (*e.g.* glass composition studies, residues in or on pottery, ceramic thin sections, and mineral-preserved organic material).

8.30 Once assessed, all material must be packed and stored in optimum conditions, as described in *First Aid for Finds* (Watkinson and Neal 1998). Waterlogged organic materials must be dealt with following *Guidelines for the care of waterlogged archaeological leather* (English Heritage/Archaeological Leather Group 1995) and *Waterlogged wood: guidelines on the recording, sampling, conservation and curation of structural wood* (Brunning 1996).

8.31 Investigative conservation will be undertaken on those objects selected during the assessment phase, with the aim of maximising information whilst minimising intervention. Where necessary, active stabilisation/ consolidation will be carried out, to ensure long-term survival of the material, but with due consideration to possible future investigations. Proposals for ultimate storage must follow *Guidelines for the Preparation of Excavation Archives for Long-Term Storage* (Walker 1990).

Analysis of technological residues, ceramics, glass and stone

8.32 Where there is evidence for industrial activity, macroscopic technological residues (or a sample of them) must be collected by hand.

8.33 Where appropriate, separate samples (*c*. 0.2 litres) must be collected for micro-slags (hammer-scale and spherical droplets).

8.34 Reference should be made to *Archaeometallurgy* (English Heritage 2001)(*cf* English Heritage 1995) and *Hammerscale* (Starley 1995).

8.35 Assessment of any technological residues will include x-radiography of a sample of industrial debris relating to metallurgy.

9. Reports

Every archaeological project will produce a report that is submitted to the LGAO and made available through the SMR/HER. These are known as 'client reports' or 'grey literature' and must contain the basic information detailed below. Some archaeological work will justify publication and this should be in a format and at a level of detail *commensurate with the results*.

This section largely refers to unpublished reports — client reports and 'grey literature'. For published reports, see 10 below.

9.1 Archaeological contractors will produce a report of *every* project undertaken for submission to the LGAO. All reports must include the results of the background research undertaken to place the evidence presented within its local and, where appropriate, its regional and/or national context, by consulting relevant Sites and Monuments Record (or equivalent) data, documents, maps and aerial photographs. All sources examined must be listed.

9.2 Reports will be rejected if it is demonstrated that they do not provide sufficient information or if they have not been compiled in accordance with the relevant sections of the Brief or this document. The reasons for rejecting any report will be stated, and contractors will be expected to revise the report and to resubmit it.

9.3 Excavation and evaluation reports submitted to the LGAO and LPA (and deposited with the project archive to the agreed place of deposition) will include, where appropriate:

- a brief non-technical executive summary of the work undertaken and the results obtained
- acknowledgements
- site details, including location, SMR/HER number, grid reference, geology, place of deposition of the archive and any relevant details of the project's history
- archaeological background, including aims and objectives
- methodology
- site narrative, comprising the detailed description, analysis and interpretation of the site or structure;
- artefactual evidence, including results of specialist reports
- environmental evidence, including results of specialist reports
- archaeological science reports, including results specialist reports
- documentary and cartographic evidence
- discussion/conclusions
- recommendations as a separate section, if included (*nb* some LGAOs will not accept a report which includes recommendations for further work)(*cf* 9.17)
- bibliography
- illustrative material including maps, plans, elevation drawings, sections, appropriate detail drawings and a key to any conventions used
- photographs, where appropriate
- lists of contexts and finds, as appendices
- specialist reports in full, as appendices
- copies of the Brief and Project Design, where required, as appendices.

9.4 Within the time specified by the LGAO a timetable for post-excavation work will be produced, following consultation, (including team meetings for larger-scale sites) with all specialists involved in the project. Timetables should be agreed in writing with external sub-contracted specialists.

9.5 Specialist reports should include details of methodology, results, interpretation and non-technical summaries.

9.6 The timetable should allow for adequate provision by the excavator of contextual information, provisional dating and stratigraphic relationships of contexts.

Project summaries

9.7 Many county journals in the region publish annual summaries of excavations and surveys, and the archaeological contractor must provide an appropriate summary/synthesis if asked to do so. The summary should contain an *irreducible minimum* of information, as defined in MAP2 Appendix 7.

Reports on Evaluations by survey and/or trial trenching

9.8 The archaeological contractor may determine the general style and format of evaluation reports.

9.9 However, the report must include an introduction with background information about the site, an outline of the development, the date of fieldwork, the personnel involved and the methodology employed. Copies of the Project Brief or Specification and Project Design must be appended, where required.

9.10 Plans at appropriate scales must be included, showing the site location, trench layout or excavation areas, finds distributions and features (by phase). Section and sample locations will be indicated. An overall site plan showing all features (hachured) must always be included.

9.11 An evaluation report must include comprehensive details of features and finds in each trench or area, their states of preservation and interpretation. Tables will summarise the recovery of finds from features within each trench or area.

9.12 An evaluation report must also include a quantification and assessment of the finds, and present an overview of the quality and potential of the finds assemblage. This should include illustrations and/or photographs of significant finds. Where appropriate, local reference collections, especially of ceramics, will be referred to for descriptive and analytical purposes in order to ensure that analysis and terminology is consistent. Relevant standards produced by national finds groups must be adhered to.

9.13 An evaluation report must include an assessment of the environmental potential of the site where this is appropriate.

9.14 Any results from assessment investigations involving archaeological science must be included in the evaluation report.

9.15 Archaeological science reports must include sufficient detail to permit the assessment of potential for analysis. They will include tabulations of data in relation to site phasing and contexts and non-technical summaries. The objective presentation of data must be clearly separated from interpretation. Any recommendations for further investigations involving archaeological science (both on samples already collected and further samples to be collected at future excavations) must be clearly separated from the results and interpretation (*cf* 9.3).

9.16 An evaluation report must include an assessment of the preservation potential of the site so that appropriate decisions can be taken about mitigation strategies.

9.17 An evaluation report will comment on the perceived effectiveness of the fieldwork in relation to the project's stated aims and objectives. It will not express an opinion on preservation or further work.

9.18 Evaluation reports must be submitted by the time specified in the Brief. This is usually on the understanding that they will become public documents after an appropriate period of time.

Reports on Area Excavations

9.19 At the Assessment stage of an excavation project an Updated Project Design must be prepared with proposals for analysis, report and publication, and agreed with the LGAO.

9.20 An excavation report must be completed and the required number of copies supplied to the relevant Sites and Monuments Record (or equivalent) within the timetable agreed with the LGAO. Programmes may be negotiated for particular projects at the Assessment stage when the analysis, report and publication timetable will be agreed with the LGAO. Where a project is phased, interim reports will be prepared and submitted on each sub-phase to an agreed timetable.

9.21 An excavation report for publication will generally include as appropriate, the following:

- title page
- list of contents, plates, figures, tables, microfiche, contributors
- acknowledgements, preface, summary
- a description of the site
- excavation methodology
- summary of phasing
- excavated features
- finds
- specialist reports
- discussion and conclusions
- appendices
- bibliography
- index
- additional material (electronic release/microfiche)

9.21 If it is intended that an excavation report will be published, refer to section 10 below.

Reports on Archaeological Monitoring and Recording (Watching Briefs)

9.22 A report on an Archaeological Monitoring and Recording Project (or Watching Brief) should be commensurate with the results.

9.23 As a minimum, it must include a one-page summary of the archaeological project, with a description of the

*... at a level of detail **commensurate** with the results*

work and any field observations, and a location plan at an appropriate scale.

Report illustrations

9.24 Where conventions are used, as is normally the case, an explanatory figure or key must be included.

9.25 All report illustrations must be fully captioned and refer to the scale of the published drawing.

9.26 Plans must be based on and indicate the National Grid, showing at least two intersections.

9.27 North must be indicated on all plans.

9.28 A bar scale must be included on all plans and sections.

9.29 Sections must indicate the alignment of the section, and the height OD of the section datum.

9.30 Plan and section illustrations must include the context numbers of all cuts, fills, layers and structures represented. The locations of significant finds and/or of samples taken will also be shown, where appropriate.

9.31 The positions of all section lines must be indicated and annotated on the appropriate plan(s).

10. Publication
by Jenny Glazebrook

The principle of replacement by record

There is extensive literature dealing with archaeological project management, in which principles and standards for field archaeology have gradually been refined (Frere 1975; Cunliffe 1982; English Heritage 1991(MAP 2); Carver *et al.* 1992). Through these documents, a management framework has been developed which emphasises selectivity and archaeological value right through to publication, and is intended to work alongside academic priorities such as those embodied in the regional research framework.

Traditionally, archaeological publication was based on the idea of *preservation by record*, but this concept is now understood as *replacement by record*, implying a process of transformation into knowledge rather than one of passive data storage. The management framework accepts *replacement by record* as one of the basic principles of archaeological excavation — the record being an *archive plus publication*. Because of this, the sponsor of an archaeological excavation must also pay for its replacement by record *satisfactory to the academic needs of the discipline* (Cunliffe 1990, 668).

In theory archives are publicly accessible, but in practice access — even to 'grey literature' — is often difficult or impossible and the published account forms the only easily obtainable record. It is important, therefore, that the account is published in a format likely to be acceptable to libraries and taken by as many libraries as possible.

Publication commensurate with results

Archaeological works will not always justify publication or publication at the same level of detail. Guidelines produced by the *East Anglian Archaeology* editorial committee indicate the range of outlets available and the criteria by which an appropriate level of dissemination can be judged (East Anglian Archaeology 2002).

In all cases a report is produced to guide the planning process and is made available through the SMR/HER (*cf* 9.1 above). Some work may endorse current knowledge rather than offer the potential to develop any new understanding, and this should be apparent to the archaeological contractor/consultant and LGAO at the Fieldwork phase or at latest the Assessment phase, following MAP2. An appropriate record will then comprise an archive deposited with the relevant body as defined below (section 11) and in MAP2 (5.4 and Appendix 3), plus a summary report in a local or period journal (*cf* 9.7 above).

Analysis takes place when material from the site *has the potential to contribute to the pursuit of local, regional or national research priorities* (MAP2, 6.16). Indeed, MAP2 (7.5) assumes that if a project proceeds to analysis it is with a planned publication in mind.

At this point the scope of the publication should be defined by the archaeological contractor/consultant, who should consider whether a full site report is intended, or a synthetic article on some aspect of the work, or detailed publication of material that is of *intrinsic archaeological value outside the context of the site report* — such as artefactual or environmental evidence (MAP2, 6.16).

10.1 The publication of archaeological work should reflect the significance of the data collected.

10.2 Some projects may involve more than one dissemination method, and this may not be known until the second assessment of results is carried out after analysis.

10.3 To ensure that relevant information is published in a clear, structured and user-friendly manner, site reports and articles must be subject to an *independent editorial process*. Suitable outlets provide academic vetting, copyediting, professional indexing and circulation to journals for review.

10.4 A *provisional publication synopsis* will be submitted by the archaeological contractor/consultant to an appropriate outlet(s) and to the LGAO at Updated Project Design stage (MAP2, Phase 4), when the resources needed for analysis, synthesising the research archive and publishing a report are also established.

10.5 Site reports must be compiled according to the report-writing criteria and the production standards laid out in MAP2. Suitable outlets will comply with these production standards, as their *Notes for Authors* will demonstrate, thus guaranteeing production quality.

10.6 Reports, including those for submission to county journals, must be drafted to conform to the requirements of the intended outlet. Contractors/consultants must establish contact with the journal or series editor at an early stage to obtain *Notes for Authors*, advice on the submission of synopses, and an estimate of the costs and timescale involved.

10.7 Until analysis has been completed, the exact content of the publication cannot be finalised. Any major alterations to report content should be subject to editorial approval, and a *final synopsis* should be sent to the outlet confirming the scope of the report and the intended delivery date of the draft text.

10.8 Publication costs can be more accurately established once the final text of the report has been agreed. Usually, these will include:

- copyediting
- typesetting
- origination of page layouts to camera-ready copy
- indexing
- printing
- distribution (including review copies)
- marketing.

10.9 Project Designs must confirm that the resources for editorial and reprographic work have been adequately built into the project.

Publication to an acceptable academic standard

As the amount of archaeological activity and the volume of available data rapidly increases, selectivity and a clear focus on defined issues are essential in publication, if uncritical reproduction of the archive is to be avoided.

10.10 When the report has been drafted, it should be subject to peer review by an independent academic referee.

the published report — always a cause for celebration!

The role of the independent referee, appointed by the editorial board of the outlet or the sponsor, is to ascertain:

- how far the publication reflects the stated aims of the project design
- whether the publication meets the general academic standards and priorities
- whether the proposed publication meets the requirements of the publishing body
- whether publication of the report is warranted and whether it meets professional standards.

By doing so, the referee addresses the needs of the archaeological community, the interests of the publisher and the sponsor.

The integration of published reports and project archives

As published reports become more selective and synthetic, the more they need to provide a gateway into the archive.

10.11 The published report will clearly state the location of the archive, its accession number, and details of the body responsible for its curation.

10.12 The published report will provide an index of the archive contents, method of reference between published report and archive information, and cite any material that is electronically accessible.

the ultimate deposit

11. Archives

11.1 The place of deposition of the Project Archive may have an Archaeological Collecting Policy to which all material to be deposited will have to conform. The archaeological contractor/consultant should seek advice and guidance on this at an early stage, and arrangements made before on-site works commence.

11.2 Where finds records have been computerised, the archaeological contractor/consultant will be expected to provide an electronic database to accompany the archive. This may need to be compatible with MODES and include defined units of information for each item or significant group of items. Where records have been computerised the data must also be present as hard copy in the site archive.

11.3 Minimum standards for site archives should be followed, as defined in MAP2, para. 5.4 and Appendix 3.

11.4 The following should also be adhered to: *Guidelines for the Preparation of Excavation Archives for Long-Term Storage* (Walker 1990) and *Selection, Retention and Dispersal of Archaeological Collections* (Society of Museum Archaeologists 1993, *Archaeological documentary archives* (Ferguson and Murray 1997) and *Microfilming archaeological archives* (Handley 1999).

11.5 Account must also be taken of the requirements of the place of deposition regarding the conservation, ordering, organisation, labelling, marking and storage of excavated material and the archive.

11.6 Owners of finds and records should be encouraged to donate these to the appropriate place of deposition as a matter of best practice in the public interest.

11.7 Where finds are retained by the owner and are not to be deposited with the project archive, a comprehensive record including detailed drawings, photographs and descriptions of individual finds must be included in the archive *in lieu* of the objects. The repository of any finds not included in the project archive must be indicated.

11.8 The finds and archive must be deposited within the specified time of the completion of the publication or, in certain circumstances, to an agreed timetable of a longer duration.

11.9 The integrity of the site archive must be maintained at all times.

11.10 For all projects, provision must be made for inclusion of the results in the relevant SMR/HER to meet local requirements. This will refer to the location of the archive and the relevant place of deposition accession number.

11.11 Digital archives must be prepared according to local requirements, and following the guidance in Bewley *et al.* 1998 and Richards and Robinson (eds) 2000.

11.12 It is normal practice for both the copyright and ownership of the paper and any digital archive resulting from an archaeological project to rest with the originating body (usually the archaeological contractor). The originating body will deposit the archive in a museum or other appropriate repository on the completion of the project, and normally transfers title and/or licences the use of the archive at this stage. It is advisable to document these arrangements in a written contract or agreement.

12. Project Monitoring

Archaeological advisors such as LGAOs undertake the important role of monitoring the quality of archaeological work. In this they are assisted by the broad frameworks provided by nationally agreed standards (for example, IFA Standard and Guidance for various types of archaeological work), by regional standards (this document) and by the detailed requirements within Briefs, Specifications and Project Designs for specific archaeological tasks.

12.1 The LGAO or his or her representative will be responsible for monitoring progress and standards throughout the project on behalf of the Local Planning Authority.

12.2 Regular monitoring by the LGAO of a project is seen as a necessary, constructive and desirable process, to ensure that satisfactory progress is being made and standards adhered to.

12.3 When the project is underway, the LGAO (acting on behalf of the relevant LPA) will review progress to ensure that:

- the development itself conforms to the submitted plans and drawings on which the archaeological Brief (and any requirement for archaeological investigation) was based
- the archaeological requirements of the Brief or Specification are being met
- the Project Design is being adhered to.

12.4 Monitoring intervals will vary according to the nature of the site and the scale of the project. The timing and frequency of monitoring points should be agreed with the LGAO. They may include the following stages:

- topsoil stripping
- during evaluation/excavation (frequency to be agreed)

- completion of evaluation/excavation
- completion of assessment
- during analysis
- completion of analysis
- submission of report and archive.

12.5 Archaeological contractors/consultants should give the LGAO not less than one week's written notice of the commencement of the work and its duration, so that arrangements for monitoring can be made. Failure to give due notice may result in trenches having to be left open until the LGAO is able to visit, and the archaeological contractor/consultant should advise any client hoping to accelerate the programme that this may be necessary.

12.6 Access to the site should be granted to the LGAO as the representative of the Local Planning Authority, to monitor the archaeological works at agreed points in the programme or at random, to ensure that these are being undertaken to professional standards and in accordance with any planning conditions or legal agreements.

12.7 The LGAO has responsibility for his/her own welfare, and will provide his/her own personal protective equipment for use during monitoring, and will inform themselves of the basic procedures for entering a site safely.

12.8 Once the fieldwork is completed, the LGAO should be closely involved with the assessment phase of the project and the preparation by the archaeological contractor/consultant of the Updated Project Design and, later still, the post-excavation stages of analysis, report and publication (if appropriate). The preparation and deposition of the project archive will also be subject to review by the LGAO and/or by the intended place of deposition.

Appendix 1. ALGAOEE Contacts

BEDFORDSHIRE
Martin Oake
Heritage and Environment Section
Culture and Environment Group
Bedfordshire County Council
County Hall
Cauldwell Street
Bedford MK42 9AP
Tel: 01234 228074
Fax: 01234 228946
Email: oakem@deed.bedfordshire.gov.uk

CAMBRIDGESHIRE
Tim Reynolds
County Archaeology Office
Cambridgeshire County Council
ELH Box 1108
Castle Court
Shire Hall
Cambridge CB3 0AP
Tel: 01223 717078
Fax: 01223 362425
Email: tim.reynolds@cambridgeshire.gov.uk

COLCHESTER
Philip Wise
Colchester Borough Council Museum Service
Museum Resource Centre
14 Ryegate Road
Colchester CO1 1YG
Tel: 01206 712222
Fax: 01206 282925
Email: philip.wise@colchester.gov.uk

ENGLISH HERITAGE EAST OF ENGLAND REGION
Brooklands House
24 Brooklands Avenue
Cambridge CB2 2BU
Tel: 01223 582700
Fax: 01223 582701

ENGLISH HERITAGE REGIONAL ADVISER FOR
ARCHAEOLOGICAL SCIENCE
Peter Murphy
Brooklands House
24 Brooklands Avenue
Cambridge CB2 2BU
Tel: 01223 582759
Fax: 01223 582701
Email: peter.murphy@english-heritage.org.uk

ESSEX
David Buckley
Heritage Conservation Manager
Heritage Conservation Branch
Waste, Recycling and Environment
Essex County Council
County Hall
Chelmsford CM1 1QH
Tel: 01245 437514
Fax: 01245 258353
Email: david.buckley@essexcc.gov.uk

HERTFORDSHIRE
Stewart Bryant
County Archaeologist
Environment Department
Hertfordshire County Council
County Hall
Hertford SG13 8DN
Tel: 01992 555244
Fax: 01992 555251
Email: stewart_bryant@hertscc.gov.uk

LUTON
Ismail Mohammed
Principal Planning Officer
Regeneration Service Planning and Development Department
Planning Division
Luton Borough Council
Town Hall
Luton LU1 2BQ
Tel: 01582 546548
Fax: 01582 547138

NORFOLK
Brian Ayers
Archaeology and Environment
Norfolk Museums and Archaeology Service
The Shirehall
Market Avenue
Norwich NR1 3JQ
Tel: 01603 493669
Fax: 01603 493651
Email: brian.ayers@norfolk.gov.uk

PETERBOROUGH
Ben Robinson
Archaeological Officer
Planning Department
Peterborough City Council
Norwich Union House
22 Church Street
Peterborough PE1 1HZ
Tel: 01733 343329
Fax: 01733 341928
Email: ben.robinson@peterborough.gov.uk

ST ALBANS
Ros Niblett
District Archaeologist
Planning and Heritage Department
City and District of St Albans
Civic Centre
St Albans AL1 3JE
Tel: 01727 819252
Fax: 01727 863282
Email: r.niblett@stalbans.gov.uk

SOUTHEND-ON-SEA
Martin Scott
Southend-on-Sea Borough Council
Civic Centre
Victoria Avenue
Southend-on-Sea SS2 6ER
Tel: 01702 215330
Email: martinscott@southend.gov.uk

SUFFOLK
Keith Wade
Archaeological Service Manager
Environment and Transport Department
Suffolk County Council
St Edmund House
County Hall
Ipswich IP4 1LZ
Tel: 01473 583288
Fax: 01473 288221
Email: keith.wade@et.suffolkcc.gov.uk

THURROCK
Annette Reeves
Senior Planning Officer (Conservation)
Thurrock Council
Civic Offices
New Road
Grays
Essex RM17 6SL
Tel: 01375 652275
Email: areeves@thurrock.gov.uk

Appendix 2. Definitions

Appraisal. A rapid examination of existing records to identify whether a development proposal has a potential archaeological dimension requiring further clarification. This is undertaken by the LGAO.

Archaeological Consultant. An archaeologist or archaeological organisation usually acting on behalf of the client (in the planning process), and who may themselves draw up a Project Design or Specification for approval by the LGAO, scrutinise and advise on the costs of an archaeological project, and monitor work for the client.

Archaeological Contractor. An archaeological organisation (unit, trust etc) usually able to provide a wide range of services, including desk-based assessments, surveys, evaluations, excavations, building recording, assessments of potential for analysis, analysis, conservation, report preparation, dissemination and the organisation and deposition of a project archive.

Archaeological Desk-Based Assessment. A programme of assessment of the known or potential archaeological resource within a specified area on land, inter-tidal zone, or underwater. It consists of a collation of existing written, graphic, photographic and electronic information in order to identify the likely character, extent, quality and worth of the known or potential archaeological resource in a local, regional, national or international context, as appropriate (IFA 1999a).

Archaeological Monitoring and Recording (sometimes referred to as an Archaeological Watching Brief) may be defined as a formal programme of observation and investigation conducted during any operation carried out for non-archaeological reasons. This will be within a specified area or site on land, inter-tidal zone or underwater, where there is a possibility that archaeological deposits may be disturbed or destroyed. The programme will result in a report and ordered archive (IFA 1999c).

Brief. An outline or framework of the planning and archaeological situation that has to be addressed, together with an indication of the scope of works that will be required. This is provided by the LGAO and is the document required by archaeological contractors to prepare a Project Design. For model briefs, see Association of County Archaeological Officers 1993.

Evaluation. Evaluation techniques are employed prior to the determination of planning applications to clarify understanding of the character, extent, and importance of archaeological remains, usually comprising a programme of non-intrusive and/or intrusive fieldwork required prior to the determination of a planning application. It will be designed to supplement and improve existing information to a level of confidence at which the archaeological potential of a site can be assessed, and so that informed and reasonable planning recommendations and decisions can then be made.

An evaluation is intended to determine the presence or absence of archaeological features, structures, deposits, artefacts or ecofacts, within a specified area on land, inter-tidal zone or underwater. If such archaeological remains are present, field evaluation defines their character, extent, quality and state of preservation, and enables an assessment of their worth in a local, regional, national or international context, as appropriate (IFA 1999b).

Evaluation techniques may include fieldwalking, metal-detecting, geophysical survey, earthwork survey, trial trenching or environmental sampling.

Excavation. An Excavation may be required where it has been decided, usually following evaluation, that any archaeological remains do not warrant physical preservation *in situ,* and that an acceptable mitigation strategy is for these to be excavated archaeologically, replaced by record, assessed, analysed, archived and a synthesis of the results disseminated.

An excavation may be defined as a programme of controlled, intrusive fieldwork with defined research objectives which examines, records and interprets archaeological deposits, features and structures and, as appropriate, retrieves artefacts, ecofacts and other remains within a specified area or site on land, inter-tidal zone or underwater. The records made and objects gathered during fieldwork are studies, and the results of that study published in detail appropriate to the Project Design (IFA 1999d).

Historic Environment Record (HER). An Historic Environment Record provides access to a comprehensive and dynamic information resource about the historic environment of its local area for public benefit and use. The historic environment includes all aspects of our surroundings that have been built, formed or influenced by human activities from earliest to most recent times.

An Historic Environment Record makes information widely accessible to specialists and to the public, managing its services and data in accordance with agreed national and international standards and guidance on best practice.

The purpose of an Historic Environment Record is to:

- advance research and new understanding about the historic environment

- inform care of the historic environment through conservation and environmental enhancement programmes and projects, state of the environment reports, and by raising public awareness about conservation needs

- inform policies and decision-making in land-use planning, development control, statutory undertakings, agri-environment and forestry schemes

- contribute to educational programmes and projects about the historic environment

- encourage public and community participation in the appreciation and enjoyment of the historic environment.

Local Government Archaeological Officer (LGAO). The Local Government Officer at County, District or Unitary Authority level who is appropriately qualified and experienced (IFA Membership and adherence to IFA's Codes of Conduct (IFA 1997a, 1997b) and formally adopted by-laws, guidelines and other relevant codes, standards and guidance documents, are regarded as baseline standards and yardsticks of competence and good operating practice).

The LGAO is responsible for the provision of archaeological services, usually including a Sites and Monuments Record or Historic Environment Record, planning policy, advice to developers, landowners, Local Planning Authorities and other agencies on the archaeological implications of planning applications and other development and land-use proposals, management of the archaeological resource, advice, education and promotion. Throughout these *Standards*, the term is taken to include other officers working under his or her authority.

The IFA is currently developing *Standards and Guidance for Curatorial Practice*, and it is naturally assumed that these will be regarded as further indicators of good operating practice that LGAOs and other curatorial archaeologists will adhere to.

Mitigation Strategy. Once the results of an evaluation are available and if a planning permission is granted, a mitigation strategy will seek to safeguard the archaeological remains. This might be achieved by the sympathetic design of foundations in order to preserve remains *in situ* or the exclusion of defined areas from further disturbance. Where this is not possible a further option is the implementation of a programme of archaeological work to excavate and 'replace by record'.

Post-excavation. A term often used to refer to the office- or laboratory-based activities of an Archaeological Contractor (and others, *e.g.* specialists) that take place after the fieldwork phase of a project. Post-excavation will usually include the assessment of potential for analysis, analysis, conservation, report preparation, dissemination and the organisation and deposition of a project archive.

Project Design (which may also be called a Method Statement or Written Scheme of Investigations). This is the document prepared by the Archaeological Contractor in response to the Brief or Specification prepared by the LGAO.

Sites and Monuments Record (SMR). An SMR is defined as: *a definitive permanent general record of the local historic environment in its national context, publicly and professionally maintained, whose data is accessible and retrievable for a wide range of purposes.* The SMR for a particular authority (county or district) is generally maintained by the LGAO or in some cases a local museum. The SMR will contain the data upon which the known archaeology (or the archaeological potential of an area) is assessed by the LGAO, and the SMR will also receive the results of archaeological fieldwork at the conclusion of a project. SMRs are increasingly collecting and holding a wider range of data on the historic environment, and developing into Historic Environment Records (HERs).

Specification. A schedule of works in sufficient detail to be quantifiable, implemented and monitored. Where a Specification is necessary or desirable this is provided by the LGAO and, like a Brief, is used by the Archaeological Contractor to prepare a Project Design.

For model specifications, see Association of County Archaeological Officers 1993.

References

Association of County Archaeological Officers, 1993
Model Briefs and Specifications for Archaeological Assessments and Field Evaluations (Bedford)

Association of County Archaeological Officers, 1997
Analysis and recording for the conservation and control of works to historic buildings

Association of Local Government Archaeological Officers East of England Regional Committee, 2000
Taking a Lead in Safeguarding the Historic Environment of the East of England

Association of Local Government Archaeological Officers, 2001
Strategy 2001–2006

Barber. J., 1993
Interpreting Stratigraphy. Proceedings of the Second Stratigraphy Conference, Edinburgh, (AOC (Scotland) Ltd)

Bewley, R., Donaghue, D., Gaffney, V., van Leusen, M. and Wise, A., 1998
Archiving Aerial Photography and Remote Sensing Data: a Guide to Good Practice, (Arts and Humanities Data Service)

Brown, N. and Glazebrook, J. (eds), 2000
Research and Archaeology: a Framework for the Eastern Counties 2. Research Agenda and Strategy, E. Anglian Archaeol. Occ. Pap. 8

Brunning, R., 1996
Waterlogged wood. Guidelines on the recording, sampling, conservation and curation of waterlogged wood, (London: English Heritage)

Campling, N., 1999
Which Archaeologist? Best Practice for Curatorial or Commissioning Archaeologists, (Association of Local Government Archaeological Officers Briefing Note)

Canti, M., 1996
Guidelines for carrying out Assessments in Geoarchaeology, English Heritage Ancient Monuments Laboratory Report 34/96 (London)

Carver, M.O.H., 1987 *Underneath English Towns,* (London)

Carver, M.O.H., 1990 'Digging for data: archaeological approaches to data definition, acquisition and analysis' in Francovich, R. and Manacorda, D. (acd) *Lo Scavo Archeologico: dalla diagnosi all'edizione,* 45–120 (Firenze: All'Insegno del Giglio)

Carver, M.O.H., Chapman, H., Cunliffe, B., Hassall, T., Hebditch, M., Lawson, A., Longworth, I., Morris, R., Phillipson, D., Schofield, J. and Wainwright, G., 1992
Archaeological publication, archives and collections: towards a national policy, (Society of Antiquaries, unpublished)

Chadwick, A.M., 1997
'Archaeology at the edge of chaos. Further towards reflexive excavation methodology', *Assemblage* 3, Worldwide Web: http://www.shef.ac.uk/~assem/3/3chad.htm

Confederation of British Industry, 1991
Archaeological Investigations Code of Practice for Mineral Operators

Corfield, M., Hinton P., Nixon, T. and Pollard, M. (eds), 1996
Preserving archaeological remains in situ: proceedings of the conference of 1st–3rd April 1996, (London: Museum of London Archaeology Service)

Council for British Archaeology, 1995
Aerial Archaeology Guidance Note

Council for the Care of Churches, 1999
'Appendix 3. Draft guidelines for the treatment of human remains' and 'Appendix 4. The Vermilion Accord' in *Church archaeology: its care and management. A report to the council from the Archaeology Working Group,* (London)

Cunliffe, B., 1982
The Publication of Archaeological Excavations, (Council for British Archaeology and the Department of the Environment)

Cunliffe, B., 1990
'Publishing in the City', *Antiquity* 64, 667–71

David, A., 1995
Geophysical survey in archaeological field evaluation, English Heritage Research and Professional Services Guideline No. 1

Department of the Environment, 1990
Planning Policy Guidance Note 16: Archaeology and Planning, (HMSO)

Department of the Environment and the Department of National Heritage, 1994
Planning Policy Guidance Note 15: Planning and the Historic Environment, (HMSO)

Department of the Environment and the Welsh Office 1992
Planning Policy Guidance Note 20: Coastal Planning

East Anglian Archaeology, 2002
Notes for Authors, 4th edition; *Submissions* and *About the Series,* http://www.eaareports.org.uk/editorial/ (E. Anglian Archaeol. Editorial Committee)

English Heritage, 1991
Management of Archaeological Projects, 2nd edition

English Heritage, 1995
Archaeometallurgy in archaeological projects

English Heritage, 1998
Monuments of War. The evaluation, recording and management of twentieth-century military sites

English Heritage, 2001
Archaeometallurgy (Centre for Archaeology Guidelines)

English Heritage, 2002
Environmental Archaeology. A guide to the theory and practice of methods, from sampling and recovery to post-excavation (Centre for Archaeology Guidelines)

English Heritage, n.d.
Minimum Standards for MAP2 Project Designs and Assessments: supplementary guidance to MAP2

English Heritage/ Archaeological Leather Group, 1995
Guidelines for the care of waterlogged archaeological leather

English Heritage/ Royal Commission on the Historical

Monuments of England, 1996 — *England's coastal heritage: a statement on the management of coastal archaeology*

Ferguson, L.M. and Murray, D.M., 1997 — *Archaeological documentary archives,* Institute of Field Archaeologists Paper No. 1

Frere, S., 1975 — *Principles of Publication in Rescue Archaeology,* (Ancient Monuments Board for England Committee for Rescue Archaeology)

Gaffney, C., Gater, J. and Ovenden, S., 2002 — *The Use of Geophysical Techniques in Archaeological Evaluations,* Institute of Field Archaeologists Paper No. 6

Glazebrook, J. (ed), 1997 — *Research and Archaeology: a Framework for the Eastern Counties, 1. Resource assessment,* E. Anglian Archaeol. Occ. Pap. 3

Handley, M., 1999 — *Microfilming archaeological archives,* Institute of Field Archaeologists Paper No. 2

Harris, E.C., 1975 — 'The stratigraphic sequence: a question of time', *World Archaeology* 7, 109–121

Harris, E.C., 1979 — *Principles of Archaeological Stratigraphy,* 1st edition (London: Academic Press)

Harris, E.C., 1984 — 'The analysis of multilinear stratigraphic sequences', *Scottish Archaeol. Rev.* 3, 127–33

Harris, E.C., Brown III, M.R. and Brown, G.J. (eds), 1993 — *Practices of Archaeological Stratigraphy,* (London: Academic Press)

Hey, G. and Lacey, M., 2001 — *Evaluation of Archaeological Decision-making Processes and Sampling Strategies,* (Planarch Project: Kent County Council)

Hillam, J., 1998 — *Dendrochonology: guidelines on producing and interpreting dendrochronological data,* (London: English Heritage)

Institute of Field Archaeologists, 1997a — *Code of Conduct,* (Revised edition)

Institute of Field Archaeologists, 1997b — *Code of approved practice for the regulation of contractual arrangements in field archaeology,* (Revised edition)

Institute of Field Archaeologists, 1998 — 'Draft principles of conduct for archaeologists involved in commercial archaeological work', *The Archaeologist* 32 (Summer 1998), 13

Institute of Field Archaeologists, 1999a — *Standard and Guidance for archaeological desk-based assessment,* (Revised)

Institute of Field Archaeologists, 1999b — *Standard and Guidance for archaeological field evaluation,* (Revised)

Institute of Field Archaeologists, 1999c — *Standard and Guidance for an archaeological watching brief,* (Revised)

Institute of Field Archaeologists, 1999d — *Standard and Guidance for archaeological excavation,* (Revised)

Institute of Field Archaeologists, 1999e — *Standard and Guidance for the archaeological investigation and recording of standing buildings or structures,* (Revised)

Institute of Field Archaeologists, 2001 — *Standard and Guidance for the collection, documentation, conservation and research of archaeological materials*

Joint Nautical Archaeology Policy Committee, 1995 — *Code of Practice for Seabed Developers*

McKinley, J. and Roberts, C., 1993 — *Excavation and post-excavation treatment of cremated and inhumed human remains,* Institute of Field Archaeologists Technical Pap. 13

Norfolk Landscape Archaeology, 1998 — *County Standards for Field Archaeology in Norfolk* (Norfolk Museums and Archaeology Service, unpublished)

Office of the Deputy Prime Minister, 2000 — *Regional Planning Guidance for East Anglia to 2016 (RPG6)*

Office of the Deputy Prime Minister, 2001 — *Regional Planning Guidance for the South East (RPG9)*

Office of the Deputy Prime Minister, forthcoming — *Planning Policy Statement 15: Planning for the Historic Environment*

Palmer, R. and Cox, C., 1993 — *Uses of Aerial Photography in Archaeological Evaluations,* Institute of Field Archaeologists Technical Pap. 12

Richards, J. and Robinson, D. (eds), 2000 — *Digital Archives from Excavation and Fieldwork: Guide to Good Practice,* 2nd edition, (Arts and Humanities Data Service)

Roskams, S. (ed), 1998 — *Interpreting Stratigraphy 8: Papers Presented to the Eighth Stratigraphy Conference at York,* (York: York Archaeological Publications)

Roskams, S. (ed), 2000 — *Interpreting Stratigraphy: site evaluation, recording procedures and stratigraphic analysis,* Brit. Archaeol. Rep. S910

Roskams, S., 2001 — *Excavation,* (Cambridge University Press)

Royal Commission on the Historical Monuments of England, 1996 — *Recording Historic Buildings; A Descriptive Specification,* 3rd edition

Royal Commission on the Historical Monuments of England, 1999 — *Recording Archaeological Field Monuments; A Descriptive Specification*

Schmidt, A., 2001 — *Geophysical Data in Archaeology: A Guide to Good Practice,* (Arts and Humanities Data Service)

Shepherd, L., 1995 — *Interpreting Stratigraphy: Proceedings of the Fifth Stratigraphy Conference, Norwich,* (Interpreting Stratigraphy 5)

Society of Museum Archaeologists, 1993 — *Selection, retention and dispersal of archaeological collections. Guidelines for use in England, Northern Ireland, Scotland and Wales,* (London)

Spence, C. (ed.), 1990 — *Archaeological Site Manual,* 2nd edition, (Museum of London)

Spence, C. (ed.), 1994 — *Archaeological Site Manual,* 3rd edition, (Museum of London)

Standing Conference of Archaeological Unit Managers, 1996 — *Guidelines and notes on competitive tendering for archaeological services*

Standing Conference of

Archaeological Unit Managers, 1997 — *Health and safety in field archaeology,* 3rd edition

Starley, D., 1995 — *Hammerscale,* Historical Metallurgy Society: Archaeology Datasheet No. 10

Steane, K. (ed), 1992 — *Interpretation of Stratigraphy: A Review of the Art. Proceedings of the First Stratigraphy Conference, Lincoln,* (City of Lincoln Archaeology Unit)

Study Group for Roman Pottery, 1994 — *Guidelines Advisory Document 1. Guidelines for the Archiving of Roman Pottery*

Study Group for Roman Pottery, 1997 — *Research Frameworks for the Study of Roman Pottery*

Thorpe, R., 1998 — 'Which Way is up? Context formation and transformation: the life and deaths of a hot bath in Beirut', *Assemblage* 2, Worldwide Web: http://www.shef.ac.uk/assem/4/4rxt.html

Trow, S. and Murphy, P., forthcoming — *Coastal Defence and the Historic Environment: a Policy Statement,* (London: English Heritage)

Walker, K., 1990 — *Guidelines for the preparation of excavation archives for long-term storage,* (Archaeology Section of the United Kingdom Institute for Conservation)

Watkinson, D. and Neal, V., 1998 — *First Aid for Finds,* 3rd edition, (RESCUE and Archaeology Section of the United Kingdom Institute for Conservation)

Williams, J. and Brown, N. (eds), 1999 — *An Archaeological Research Framework for the Greater Thames Estuary,* (Essex County Council)

Index

access 12
aerial photography 11
amateur archaeology 2, 12
animal bones 17
appraisal 26
archaeological consultants/contractors 7, 25
archives 21
Association of Local Government Archaeological Officers for the East of England 1, 2, 23–4

building recording 6, 14–15
burials 12, 17

cemeteries 12, 17
ceramics 17
conservation 11, 15, 17
Conservation Areas 9
Countryside Stewardship Schemes 9
county journals 18

dating 12, 16
definitions 25–6
dendrochronology 16
desk-based research 9–10, 25

education 2
English Heritage 3
environmental data 11, 12, 16–17
Environmental Impact Assessment Directives and Regulations 3
Environmentally Sensitive Areas 9
evaluation 6, 12, 13, 18–19, 25
excavation 6, 11–12, 19, 25

fieldwalking *see* surveys
finds 11, 15, 17

geoarchaeology 16
geophysical surveys *see* surveys
glass 17

health and safety 8–9
historic buildings 3–4
Historic Environment Impact Assessment 4
Historic Environment Records 2, 6, 9, 25
human remains 12, 17

illustrations 19
Institute of Field Archaeologists 1, 7, 8

listed buildings 3, 9
Local Government Archaeological Officers 6–7, 8–9, 25–6
Local Plans 4

macrofossils 16
Management of Archaeological Projects 7, 8
marine archaeology 3
metal-detecting *see* surveys
microfossils 16
mineral sites 3
mitigation strategy 26
monitoring and recording *see* watching briefs

National Association of Local Government Archaeological Officers 1
National Monuments Record 6

planning conditions 3, 6

planning guidance
    Planning Policy Guidance 15 3–4
    Planning Policy Guidance 16 3, 4
    Planning Policy Statement 15 4
    regional and local 4
planning procedures 6–7
    flow chart 5
pottery *see* ceramics
preservation *in situ* 14
professional values 2
Project Designs 1, 7, 8–9, 26
project monitoring 22
Project Specifications 1, 7, 8, 26
project summaries 18
publication 2, 6, 19–21

Regional Action Plan 1
Regional Advisors for Archaeological Science 12
Regional Planning Policy Guidance 4
Regional Standards
    archaeological science 15–17
    archives 21
    desk-based research 9–10
    development of 1–2
    finds and conservation 15, 17
    general requirements 8–9
    intrusive methodologies 11–13
    non-intrusive surveys 10–11
    project monitoring 22
    publication 19–21
    reports 17–19
    standing structures 14–15
    urban archaeology 13–14
reports 17–19
Research Frameworks 1
Risk Assessments 8–9

sampling 12, 13, 16
Scheduled Monuments 3, 9
seabed developments 3
sieving 12, 16
Sites and Monuments Records 2, 6, 9, 19, 26
Sites of Special Scientific Interest 9
specialists 15
Standing Structure Impact Assessment 4
stone objects 17
Structure Plans 4
surveys, non-intrusive 10
    aerial photographic surveys 11
    earthwork surveys 10–11
    fieldwalking 10
    geophysical 11, 15–16
    metal-detecting 10
    reports 18–19

technological residues 17
tendering 7
Treasure Act 10, 15
Tree Preservation Orders 9
trial-trenching 12, 18–19

underwater archaeology 3
Urban Archaeological Databases 2, 6
urban archaeology 13–14

watching briefs (monitoring and recording) 6, 13, 19, 25